The Great Collaboration

Also by Naoya Fujiwara:

(Recent books in Japanese)
Collapse of the Nation: The Final Chapter
The World Simultaneous Great Depression
Collapse of the Nation II: Who Will Survive and Who Won't
The Great Sea Change: A New Japan Emerges
Collapse of the Nation: Your Assets and Debt Will Vanish
The Quiet End of the Japanese Economy
Global Economic Blackout: Change Yourself to Be a Winner Again

The Great Collaboration

✦

A Prescription for a Healthy, Sustainable Future

Naoya Fujiwara

translated into English by Office Miyazaki Inc.

iUniverse, Inc.
New York Lincoln Shanghai

The Great Collaboration
A Prescription for a Healthy, Sustainable Future

iUniverse books may be ordered through booksellers or by contacting:

iUniverse
2021 Pine Lake Road, Suite 100
Lincoln, NE 68512
www.iuniverse.com
1-800-Authors (1-800-288-4677)

ISBN: 978-0-595-43858-7 (pbk)
ISBN: 978-0-595-88181-9 (ebk)

Printed in the United States of America

Contents

Introduction

A spectre is haunting Japan—the spectre of hope forlorn.

The optimism and self-assurance, the energy and can-do enthusiasm that carried the nation through its remarkable series of transformations in the last century seems to have vanished with the end of the Showa emperor's reign. In the late 1980s, Japan stood proud—and with justification—boasting what was arguably the most balanced and dynamic of the world's economies, its manufacturing sector dominant, its markets thriving and its populace enjoying unprecedented wealth and security.

Few at the time foresaw that within a few years the economic bubble would have broken (or even that a Bubble had formed at all). Looking back now, though, we must admit that the writing was very clearly on the wall. A simplistic faith in the sustainability of fundamentally unsustainable growth, a host of political and economic factors, both domestic and external, that militated against Japan's continued predominance and, most of all, a failure of leadership, brought the country to its knees. Stagnation, deflation and retrenchments followed, stymieing ministry officials' efforts to hoist the economy back onto the rails, sinking once-proud corporate and financial titans, and leaving the Japanese people to rummage amidst the bleak offals of a miracle economy gone bad.

The fifteen years since that wave finally crested and broke, crashing down somewhere between Kasumigaseki and Ginza and carrying the whole of the country along in the cataract, has been a time for soul-searching here in Japan. But I would argue that they also serve as warning signs, prodromal symptoms of the fundamental ill health of the global order. Japan was at the leading edge in the late 20th century, and so bore the brunt of the first wave of stark realities rushing in to fill a void that had been papered over by fictions. But the sclerosis, atrophy and crepitous unsoundness exposed by the financial meltdown circa 1991 was by no means unique to Japan, and we are now seeing a similarly untenable scenario in the making, only this time on a worldwide scale.

The prognosis admittedly seems grim, and undeniably, when the global bubble pops, the shock will be intense and the hurt deep. But I will also argue that, as for any historical inevitability, the change will represent opportunity for those who are prepared to shed the old ways and embrace a new paradigm. Evolution is adaptation. The 21st century will favor those who are able to thrive in a new order that emphasizes commitments over competition, networks of trust over concentrations of power, lifestyles of health and sustainability over dehumanization. Seen from that perspective, the cracks we are already seeing develop in the 20th century structure are frightening only if you continue to cling to the pillars of the familiar, even as they buckle and crumble down. The first question for many is how to salvage this situation, but I prefer to ask, "Is the old order worth saving? Can we not find a better way to live?"

I believe that we can. A society—what I call the Great Collaboration—can prosper and thrive, can provide all of its individuals with security, stimulation and contentment, and can serve as a model for a new way of life that, in my view, represents the only livable future for humanity. I have studied and taught political economics, I have worked in the engine rooms of global finance and witnessed firsthand the powers that drive and steer the world as it is, I have monitored the news closely for years and felt the pulse of forces that underlie the stories, and everything I know and can sense tells me that we are on the cusp of a transformation that will be cataclysmic in its scale and impact. I have written extensively on the storm that has been gathering here in Japan for more than a decade; now, in this small book, I hope to consolidate those observations and apply them to creating a model of what might be, if enough people take notice and act in time. The storm is coming; that much is certain. Whether it will bring devastation or new bounty is for us to decide.

My focus in this argument will be on Japan's experience of its own economic bubble and the societal aftermath of its massive implosion, because I believe what happened here already is now about to strike the world entire. I will also propose what I see as the possible solution to Japan's woes; again, because if it can be made to work here, it might well be the best answer to the massive instabilities, jarring incongruities and structural defects that characterize the prevailing 20th century order. So this work will take the form of a diagnosis and an indictment, a prescription and manifesto, in which Japan serves as a model for how things can go so wrong, and how, perhaps, they can be put right again.

Naoya Fujiwara

Land of the Setting Sun?

As I was writing this book, *The New York Times* (of all places!) ran a short article on a rural community on the coast of the Sea of Japan, the village of Ogama. The story reported how this tiny hamlet, left with only eight residents, all of them over 60 years old, had elected to abandon its futureless isolation and sell all of its land to a company that intends to use it as an industrial waste site. This event, which barely even registered in the Japanese media, perfectly symbolizes the tragedy of current-day Japan—tradition sacrificed to the myth of progress and its awful spawn, the hegemony of urban over rural interests, hopelessness, capitulation, scorn for the uncompetitive, and a resignation on all sides to accept darwinian vicissitudes as inevitabilities.

There's none of the satisfaction here of a David and Goliath adventure where the yeomanry rallies to save the village, its history, folkways and natural beauty, perhaps by appealing to a greater community, which joins together to respond to the call to arms to drive off the corporate giant. In a movie, that is likely how the story would end. But in Japan in the early 21st century, the reality is that Ogama has been sold for landfill and its residents, some of them older than 80, will quietly take the proceeds from the sale of their native soil and shuffle off to end their lives amid alien corn.

Ogama is not alone. Japan's rural districts from Okinawa to Hokkaido are facing similar pressures and abandonment issues. Ignored by the government, unable to participate in a globalized economy where multinational corporations and cartels leverage their size and global reach to compete any and all perceived "rivals" out of existence (rivals meaning anyone with the effrontery to be in the same business), and deprived even of hope for the future as they watch their young head off to the cities, villages across Japan are confronted with similar fates.

What could have brought us to this point, where such tragedy not only can happen, but indeed can be viewed as part of the normal scheme of things, an acceptable write-off as progress relentlessly marches on? We live in an age of collateral damage. How could the Japanese, a people whose agricultural heritage extends to the very roots of their history and culture, have come to look on the demise of their rural communities with indifference? The answer is in values, a set of values and a definition of success in which short-term profit trumps all other concerns and human suffering is just part of the cost of doing business.

Of course, it's simple to point to places where Japan has seemed to thrive under this philosophy, with the reinvention and revitalization following our defeat in World War II, which ultimately led to the manufacturing boom that propelled Japan to the highest ranks of the world's economies. The story of how the implementation of Deming's quality controls, just-in-time distribution, and the unified effort of the political, administrative and industry sectors forged Japan into a world power is already an old one, whose details can be found spelled out exhaustively in any number of books. But success can be a dangerous thing.

The story that gets told less frequently is of the price Japan has paid for those past successes, the compromises, accommodations and deferrals made along the way, a record of forfeits whose legacy lingers today and even now continues to grow. The question we need to ask ourselves is how much of our collective future have we sacrificed. You can see it in our political structure, our struggles for diplomatic legitimacy, our lopsided and lurching economy and defenseless financial systems, our demographics and urban planning—indeed, it seems nothing has escaped the 20th century taint. But what exactly is the nature of that taint? Where did the last several decades go wrong, and why have administrators and interventionists failed to rectify situations that are so obviously out of control. Before writing a prescription, first we must work out an etiology and develop a diagnosis....

A Clinical History of the Global Malaise

Tracing the current bubble economy back to its roots reveals a long and fraught back-story. After World War II, with Japan in ruins, W. Edwards Deming helped restore the Japanese economy by introducing the principles of quality control. The US provided security, resources and markets, to the extent that by the 1980s, Japanese manufacturing had become the most competitive in the world. Japanese financial institutions took that production revenue and funneled it into real estate and stocks, building up a war chest they used to finance a globetrotting spending spree, triggering panic in the States. The US played the deregulation card as a means to keep the rampant Japanese economy in check, and in the 1990s began serving up advantages and lagniappes to Japan's neighborhood rival, China, strategically setting the two Asian powers against each other.

For those readers new to economic analysis, this seems like an opportunity to introduce a fundamental principle: things are never what they seem. American politicians and policy-wonks pound tables and thunder on about free trade and the rising tide of globalization lifting boats, but there are arrières-pensées and occult agendas that shape and color every gesture and syllable. The rabbit hole is deep, dark and tortuous, twisting back through GATT, the launch of the IMF and World Bank at Bretton Woods, beyond the rigged speculators' markets that crashed in '29, beyond the shameful record of imperialism that traversed the Atlantic so neatly from Europe to the US and global business following WWI and the Treaty of Versailles, back at least to the granting of legal personhood to corporations (ironically via a perverse exegesis of the 14th Amendment, originally intended to protect freed slaves by giving them citizenship) after the American Civil War. It's always dangerous to pick up a historical thread, as it never really runs out—you could easily keep following the bread crumbs back to British colonialism, joint stock companies and the Triangle Trade, even to enclosures of village commons and the first stirrings of international commerce and banking in Renaissance Europe. It's one long jeremiad of the weaponization of money and the evil men do.

Whatever the past, by about 1995, America had begun to feel secure in the knowledge that there would be no second act for the Japanese economic miracle, and China for its part had masterfully cooked up a currency scheme that kept the *renminbi* dirt cheap in dollar terms, kicking off their present economic boom, compounded in its strength by the fact that, at the time, the Chinese government, economy and workforce was still functioning as a single, undivided entity. The result was boom-time for the Chinese mainland and expat circle of "sea turtles" that rings Southeast Asia.

But too much is never enough, and the overheating Tiger economies hit the wall in 1997 (thanks in no small part to the efforts of a gang of currency speculators led by George Soros), triggering an Asian economic crisis that shattered one country after another. Zionist money was all going to military spending, and in 1998 a Russian-German alliance staged the Russia default that came within a hair of bringing down the world's financial markets. Here now was Europe using Russia to try to squelch an American-branded world economy that had been bulldozing along since the end of the Cold War, which is certainly understandable given the US record of extortion and protectionism vis-à-vis Europe following World Wars One and Two. In an effort to recoup at least some of its astronomical losses from that near-disaster, America cooked up the dot com bubble, which disintegrated just about the time that it had made good on the previous losses.

That sent major shockwaves through both China and the US. The fearsome deity that had first reared its head in 1997 returned, as if by prophecy, in the closing year of the 20th century and began to make its true scale and scope known. But that economic reverse was too sudden for America to accept, and since entering the 21st century the government has been a house divided, and now America has resorted to fear-mongering of every sort as the sole means of retaining its hold on power. Ordinarily, a nation is supposed to allow its people to dream and empower them to turn those dreams into reality, but now in America, where both dreams and the hope needed to entertain them have been lost, the government is beginning to rule with an imperious and iron-gloved hand. But such regimes cannot last. The invasion of Iraq has been an abject failure, and with sword rattling in Iran and outbreak of total war at the Israel-Lebanon border, the Middle East as a whole seems ready to break free from its moorings.

In the Far Eastern sphere, the Chinese economic constellation was hit hard after the silicon bubble popped circa 2001, leaving them with no clear mandate to continue to steer the economy. They have now joined forces with the hapless Bush regime and, employing the same kinds of scare tactics, have begun wresting the Communist Party's power and consolidating the nation's wealth to allow them to keep the investment flowing into what has evolved into a strikingly abnormal national economy.

Back when the CCP held even tighter rein over the national enterprise, they nearly rode the Chinese economy right into the ground, and it looks like we're seeing a repeat of that, with the political leaders putting a proud face on everything while deep troubles boil just under the surface. Their previous debacle was financed by Japanese money, so at least then they were safe in the knowledge that they could default with impunity. This time, it's American and Zionist capital that has made the loans. They were surely unhappy at being shorted on the return, but just as Japan did in the 1990s, if they couldn't get their money back, at least they grabbed every last piece of the juicy low-hanging fruit within reach. The US asserted itself in the Taiwan independence movement, and since the summer of 2005 China and America have been in a wary political clench.

But the real winner in all this Sino-American maneuvering has been the Japanese manufacturing industry. A resource- and technology-hungry China has showed inflexible demand for things Japanese, and in recent years China has supplanted the US as Japan's biggest trading partner. Look out the window of an airplane crossing the Sea of Japan to Shanghai on any night and the lights of the ships below are like a star-filled sky. And though manufacturers made out nicely without having to expose themselves to the geopolitical crossfire, their success also highlights Japan's great weakness in that it has not created markets, only waited for orders to come in after others have done so. Customers, not allies. And lo, once again they're perched atop a bubble that's losing pressure precipitously. The endgame now has massive investments into facility construction, staff and subcontractors pushed past endurance and teetering on the brink of collapse. You can only bail against the tide for so long.

The rudeness that so rudely interrupted this Chinese-American courtship ironically came from an unanticipated corner, in the form of Japan's lifting of quantitative easing in the spring of 2006. In the early days of the Iraq war, there was an incident in which a single bullet from a farmer's rifle brought down an American helicopter; in bringing down the buckling fairy-castle fashioned by the US-China accord, this event is having a similarly asymmetric impact. No doubt the consequences for the BOJ will be ugly, but in the US rate hikes are causing many homeowners' mortgages to ramp up into unserviceable debt, and companies have also been feeling the hurt; the once unsinkable General Motors posted negative sales growth of 15% in March 2006, placing it toes over the line into bankruptcy. If nothing else, Bush can stand tall at least among the ranks of presidents who spent the country into record deficits—he is without a doubt a top-ranking member of that elite group, the undisputed champion. Thanks to the fresh-minted Fed chief Ben Bernanke, America's interest rates are already on the rise, and bonds, debentures and mortgage securities are all already in decline; only NYSE stocks are continuing to perform at the time of this writing, and their slide is only a matter of time.

When China and the US go down, they will go down together, like two black holes colliding, sucking in anything in their orbits and destroying everything they devour. That event will send gravitational ripples across the economic universe and the impact will be immediate, lasting and profound. But as Stephen Hawkings demonstrated, even the darkest, most destructive force in the universe is not an absolute void. In the fullness of time, even black holes emit light. And where there's light, there is hope. China and America seem destined to drag each other down in the vortex of their mutual implosion, and the world must brace itself for the turbulence ahead.

And what of Japan, suddenly finding itself tethered not to a world-beater, the bronzed and barrel-chested titan known as the United States of America, but a bloated and couch-bound has-been? Where are we now in terms of our place in the global order? The economy is being made to seem like it's finally beginning to peek out from the hole it dropped into a decade and a half ago, but how much of that is solid, and how much a sop for the masses, remains seriously in doubt. The American markets are a rigged casino engineered to maximize the addictive sense of thrill on the part of a legion of desperate gamblers, hooked on crapshoot adrenaline, where the point of the game isn't winning, it's the rush. But here we favor milder entertainments, satisfying ourselves with juggling, puppetry and shadow play from the media and money pundits. The end result is much the same—empty diversions where only a handful of players know the true rule-set and the actual stakes that are up for grabs.

How did we get in this mess, on the business end of an Anglo-Saxon vision of untrammeled conquest and plunder? Again, we can trace the history back to postwar acquiescence, suppression and appeasement, to misguided prewar adventurism and the imperial aspirations of a few branches of the military, to the day in 1863 when Perry's black ships parked themselves off the coast and introduced a new and compelling form of gunboat diplomacy to a long-insulated and isolated realm. But for our purposes, we can look to the reign of former Prime Minister Junichiro Koizumi for a neat encapsulation of the reasons.

The Koizumi Legacy

Picture a small dog, pampered, coiffed and de-clawed, a tame little pooch that sits in its master's lap and feeds on the occasional tidbit it receives for its obedience and its pleasing willingness to perform tricks and run the odd errand. The prerequisite skill set includes the ability not to yap, bite or soil the carpet. Such an animal may be prized by its owner and praised for its qualities, but it nonetheless remains a dog, less even than a servant, and certainly not asked to sit at the table when matters of import are discussed or feasts are being shared. But the lapdog's life is a good one, for a dog, but this seemingly tame house pet may suddenly turn vicious if its territory is infringed. The first allegiance of such a creature is to itself, not other less well-favored members of its own species, and it knows well how it would fare were it shut out of doors and left to fend for itself.

The unflattering image of Koizumi as a lapdog was commonly adduced in the Japanese media; unfortunately it is one he earned full well. Perhaps what is most shameful about it was that he sat at the feet of a man who himself is little more than a cavity-headed and double-jointed marionette. A servant's dog is itself a pitiable thing, but you certainly don't want one running (ruining) your country. Koizumi, his anointed cabinet and the LDP coalition he has manipulated so masterfully form a league whose mission seems focused on buying more time in power for themselves by selling off Japan's wealth to foreign government and global business interests. Little changes now that his heir Shinzo Abe has taken the throne.

This sell-off and sell-out takes many forms, made possible by the government's own efforts to accommodate the demands of globalizers, and to confront foreign pressure by collapsing at the first sign of it. Despite this solicitude, however, Japan has won itself few friends and lost most of those allies it had since the turn of the century. Once, if only for its financial might, Japan stood as a looming presence on the world stage, a bogeyman economists used to frighten their children with, bent on dominating markets and making conspicuous shows of its purchasing power, after the long Heisei slump Japan was reduced first to a shadow, then a caricature, and now a pariah that receives the kind of diplomatic treatment reserved for the indigent, enfeebled or congenitally defective.

This is not simply the bitter fruit of a sour economy. Oafish diplomacy and poor choice in friends has played a major part as well. Koizumi's dogged loyalty to Bush in the run-up to and the prosecution of the shameful assault on Iraq have made Japan something of a liability, if not persona non gratis, in most of the Middle East, a region in which it had prided itself on long and expensively cultivated good relations. The Self-Defense Forces may now be withdrawn, but the memory lingers of their cooperation as US and British troops played conquerors in a hostile occupation characterized by collateral damage; illegal detentions; the wholesale massacre of civilians; "extraordinary rendition," attack dogs and human-car battery interfaces at Abu Ghraib; and the establishment of a puppet government crippled by ethnic and sectarian strife. While we should be grateful not to have been directly involved in the killing, we can take no pride in this *soi disant* humanitarian mission when confronted with the truth. Koizumi pushed the Constitution to its limits in an embarrassing show of support for a status quo of American hegemony by the gun, volunteering Japan as cheerleader and water boy for the team that much of the world was rooting openly against.

Nearer to home, his yearly pilgrimage to the Yasukuni Shrine, repeated with calculated invidious timing on VJ Day, 2006, made it simple for what might otherwise be unpopular leaders in China and South Korea to rally their citizens against Japan at will. They should have paid his salary that month. What's tragic about his undiplomatic insistence on pushing this same button is that it never seemed to dawn on Koizumi that he had been made obsolete in his role as watchdog of the East by the new coziness in relations between China and the US. What once might have been thought of as a staunch defense seemed more like a neighborhood nuisance, a toothless old mongrel howling jealously at his master's new friend. The tacitly sanctioned territorial disputes over tiny islands and resource rights in the Sea of Japan and Taiwan Straits only strained Japan's relations with its nearest and most important neighbors even further, even as China supplanted America as Japan's number one partner in trade.

These developments were not hard to forecast or avoid, but our foreign service seemed bent on playing the hard guy to China and its Korean clients. Didn't anyone notice that America has already invited China into its circle in a gesture of, if not goodwill, at least *Realpolitik* accommodation? It's safe to say that there will be no place for house pets in closed meetings between the two. Meanwhile, populists in Beijing and Seoul get three free swings at the Japanese piñata to be taken at a time of their choosing whenever an economic downturn, social injustice, government corruption or human rights abuse might otherwise grab the public imagination. Perhaps Japan still provides a useful public service as bogeyman after all.

Fortunately, Koizumi's unconditional puppy love for things American is not shared by the average Japanese, and recently the Americans themselves have had to request that his administration tone down the more fulsome aspects of their pro-US support. The steadfast resistance to base relocations in places like Okinawa and Iwakuni has put the fear of a South Korea-style ouster into the hearts of the US policy and diplomatic corps, even as Koizumi and his Diet majority blithely ignored the signs. These, after all, were not rallies by a loose band of disreputable old lefties—these were petitions and referenda passed by long majorities and petitions and letters of protests delivered to the government in person by governors and heads of local governments. But only a swat on the nose with a rolled up issue of the *Nikkei Shimbun* from the master of the house was able to bring that to the administration's attention. (Hard as they try to please, sometimes one has to be firm.) It should be noted, however, that the Americans were less concerned with such niceties when they presented a bill for restationing the Marines in Guam, the total charge estimated somewhere in the vicinity of one trillion yen.

Not every diplomatic encounter has seen such complaisant pliability. In the standoff over beef imports, for example, the administration put up a spirited token resistance before folding like a house of cards and re-opening Japan's supermarkets and restaurants to cuts of meat that would not pass Japan's own food safety muster. The re-re-opening of the markets, however, was where they really stood tough, although frankly one suspects that by this point the Americans themselves were a bit embarrassed by the whole affair, which at any rate for them was little more than a slow news day item from the start.

The most recent test of the administration's diplomatic mettle and clout came with the test-firing of seven missiles by North Korea, one of which was a long range Taepodong-2, pointed unsubtly in the direction of Japan. It is still unclear where this was supposed to come down (some speculate near Hawaii), as it blew up within seconds after launch, but I'm certain that Kim Jong-Il has to have considered the real test a success (although he may introduce a few of the Taepodong engineers to the penal system for fouling his sales demo of a homegrown delivery system priced just right for aspiring nuclear powers). The test, of course, being the testing of the resolve of the US-Japan security pact to preserve peace, freedom, democracy and capitalism in this part of the world. Perhaps emboldened by the sheer cheek of the deed, Japan's normally timid representatives rallied, imposing economic immediate sanctions and calling for a UN Security Council-backed ban on the transfer of funds, material, or technology to the Hermit Kingdom in response. Shinzo Abe and Taro Aso both went so far as to moot the possibility of preemptive strikes (made somewhat less of a threat by the fact that Japan has no such capability at present). Russia and China, being the devout advocates of rational win-win solutions that they are, vetoed the call for sanctions and expressed instead their disappointment and regret at the test firing. North Korea meanwhile continues to show a true genius for brinkmanship and an uncanny sense of timing, with Iran simmering away and Lebanon exploding right on schedule, reducing the whole thing to a page 4 sidebar and a set of expired links within days after the event.

Is this the best our Foreign Ministry and ambassadorial corps can do? Encirclement and neutralization are not supposed to be spectator sports, particularly for governments in the affected countries. Before rushing to judgment, though, to be fair one recent triumph of international deal-making, power brokerage and consular craft needs to be recognized. After billions of yen in Overseas Development Aid and years of backroom arm-twisting, cajolery and quid pro quo, Japan's efforts have paid off in the fight over international whaling, assembling a proud coalition that included Nicaragua, Iceland, Cambodia, Palau, and Antigua to re-open the issue of possible commercial whaling in the future. Bravo! Mission accomplished. Now if they can just get people to start eating the things again ...

Given what we know about the deterioration of the geopolitical situation, however, perhaps Koizumi's foreign policy failures may be forgivable—after all, the whole global order seems destined to burn down, implode or fizzle out in the frighteningly near future, and with all the chaos in the air, perhaps its better to be free and clear of alliances today that might turn to liabilities tomorrow.

It's the Economy, Stupid(ly)

Botched diplomacy aside, the true Koizumi legacy will be his fire sale disposition of Japan's national wealth. The Koizumi "reforms" are actually quite straightforward when looked at in terms of the economy. First step: financial freewheeling on a grand scale. Take the Bank of Japan's reserves, which stand at five times the legally prescribed minimum, for starters and throw in prolonged zero percent interest rates for good measure. I think it's fair to say that this has been an unprecedented concentration of reserves by any institution, and now that hoard of cash has been unleashed into financial, real estate and overseas markets, pumping more and more air into an ever-growing bubble. Fiscal expenditures are slated to drop under the rubric of reform, but while there are sharp cuts in certain sectors, the overall picture shows little in the way of meaningful change. Somehow they've managed to tighten the fiscal belt a notch while at the same time dropping their regulatory pants to the floor. The foreign exchange situation since Koizumi's arrival in office has sent trade surpluses skyward.

In real terms as well, profits have been on the rise since 2004, meaning that somebody seems to be intent on making sure that the yen punches below its weight. A booming China and the shoring up of the competitiveness of other Japanese industries are factors, no doubt, but ensuring that it remains possible to keep cashing in on the American auto market is the major impetus behind Point 2 of the Koizumi game plan: Keep the yen cheap. There's a lot of talk about how the *renminbi* is undervalued, with decibel levels rising dramatically following the transition from a China-friendly Clinton to a pro-Japan Bush, and any move to upwardly revaluate the yen just seem to keep getting lost in the ruckus. The reality of the economy under the Koizumi reforms, which are still unspooling even after his departure last fall, is a hell-bent-for-leather push by policy and industry wonks to relax financial strictures and suppress the yen's value, which is all well and good for solid companies and capable individuals, who are sure to make the most out of any situation they find themselves in, but for everyone else, the net effect will be a transient blip of easy cash flow with money flurrying in from stock transactions and real estate speculation for a short time. But once those magic deregulatory pills run out, there'll be nothing left to show for it once the dust settles.

Meanwhile, the numbers keep getting worse in America's immensely lopsided trade imbalance with China, and now that the Chinese government has managed to erect a system for the completely discretionary selling off of dollars, China has set itself up as a potentially extremely dangerous virtual foe to the States, which would have deep and potentially life-threatening consequences for Japan as we know it. If China were to opt suddenly to buy a large amount of American bonds, it could send US interest rates plunging, while a major bond sell-off would have an equal effect in the opposite direction. This kind of economic cage rattling can be achieved simply by buying up and selling off in huge quantities, over and over again, destabilizing markets through repeated dizzying drops and rises that act like a series of tsunamis that wash over the markets, carrying before them on a path to destruction both those involved in the market, and the people of the affected country itself.

If that were to happen, the damage to the US and the world financial markets (including the Nikkei) it drives would be as great as an Al Qaeda attack or an atomic bomb. Here's the key to America's global hegemony through market economics: the whole free market system is based on the principle that no one will go against the American political system and everyone will adhere to the same set of Anglo-Saxon legalistic rules; the system only functions when that is true. America's domination of the world can only work through a two-sided cooperation where one hand keeps pointing out that markets need to be left open while the other slyly manipulates the politics and laws in other countries to its own best advantage. That's the secret of America's double standard of freedom and enforcement. And with Japan's government lashed to the American mast, it's clear what will happen when the boat finally swamps.

It's interesting how this implicit influence shows up, for example, in US government demands of Japan, such as calls for more members of the Fair Trade Commission here to study more economics, and to include more grads in international finance, highlighting the fact that the current economics curriculum has slyly been co-opted as a tool of American dominion, and the reason why the US wants people who've absorbed that dogma right into the marrow of their bones at the regulatory front lines (read, Heizo Takenaka et al.).

With suborned agencies in countries around the world unwilling to go against the American line, the US became able to play the markets for profit. America may have mastered both the legal and political systems in Japan, but Russia broke ranks by defaulting on its debts in 1998, and of course China has refused to play along right from the get-go. It would have made sense to get this dangerous development under control, but the lure of easy money drew America ever deeper into China, handing more and more dollars over to the Chinese government in what's now shaping up into a blunder of historic proportions. China now has the power, both *de jure* and *de facto*, to topple America at its pleasure. China is enjoying the fact that it has the US at its mercy, and that the US is in a slack-jawed panic in the knowledge that it has lost a trump card now that China can steer the dollar's value at will through its foreign reserves. But rather than using their new-found power to shake America till parts start falling off, this alliance of the military and the wealth-holders is more likely to make use of that demonstrable might more subtly to consolidate their power base at home. Watch for suppression at home and jingoism abroad—it looks like China is headed straight into a new Cultural Revolution.

What will all this mean here in Japan? First off, everything made in China will become more expensive. That means that some products will be selected right out of price competition, which should help drive up the prices of domestic goods. The floating of the renminbi is another factor that will accelerate inflation at home. The moony infatuation with China on the part of Japanese companies will also enter a cooling off phase, and by my reckoning we'll see an end to the days when China could expect to watch the yen roll in without so much as a "thank you ma'am." But the case remains that there are long stretches of coastal China (think Dalian) where the economy and local employment are still driven by Japanese industry, and no matter how imperious the Beijing government becomes, there will be many on the coasts who want to maintain good relations with Japan, a reality much the same as the need for the American West Coast to retain its strong ties with Asia would be if the US government should manage to tank the rest of the country; we're standing on the threshold of a new Pacific economy.

As for the domestic economy circa mid-2006, they say the job market is finally stabilizing, but the truth of the matter is the ranks of the unemployed are swelling. Lots of people are realizing there's no good work to be had and have given up looking altogether, de-qualifying them as official jobless, which means they no longer show up when the unemployed headcount is made. The unemployed statistically transmogrified into the disappeared.

We can already see what Act Five of the tragedy known as the Koizumi reforms will bring—a lemming stampede by the bureaucratic-industrial complex. The coming storm is going to flatten the unlucky, and leave many households bereft. These are reforms that make clawing your way back up an individual responsibility. The whole edifice is leaning on the crutches of loosey-goosey fiscal regulation and a cheap yen, but when those props are gone, that will spell the end of glomming off the financial markets (meaning zero interest, speculative trading, REITs—the whole shebang) and export trade.

Japan has enjoyed bedrock social protections for a half-century now, but even those are under attack. If you asked me whether you can expect to receive a pension when you retire, the answer would still be yes, but if you asked whether you'd be able to survive on it, the sad but emphatic answer would be no. The coming pension crisis is shared by every advanced nation, and none of them has arrived at a workable solution. Get ready for the modern version of *ubasuteyama*, a legendary mountain where the old and feeble were taken to die of exposure. The trend is for decreased involvement by government and industry, no interest guarantees and a general shift toward an emphasis on individual responsibility in the planning and management of pension schemes, with governments providing only the barest minimum in welfare. This represents a deviation from the principles of the welfare state and one that has yet to be either widely discussed or sanctioned by the public at large. If pension plans continue to be run as they are today, it will bankrupt the national coffers, bring down companies, and ultimately leave individual pensioners without support. But no effort is being made to resume these lapsed covenants of social welfare and protections; just keep shifting the whole burden onto the individual, and let the chips fall where they may in a game of Darwinian survival.

In countries of Anglo-Saxon heritage, organized under the core principles of British and American law, the definition of the nation differs from that in countries such as Japan, which follow a Continental model of government, where the people and the governing body are distinct, partners in a contractual agreement in which each has its own rights and responsibilities. Under this model, the failure to honor its pension commitments is construed as a breach of contract on the part of the governing body, sufficient to occasion a revisit to the terms of the entire compact, just as might happen following a defeat in war or the inability of the government to provide for the safety of the people. Under the Anglo-American model, pensions are fundamental to the polity, and the handling of these pension crises will bear close watching. Under the influence of American and England, Japan is also changing with the generation born immediately after the war moving closer to a cold view of the relationship between public and government defined as a set of contractual rights and obligations. It will be interesting to see how members of the postwar generation, who have been promised and expect to receive pensions, will respond when they're told that the system is out of money when they reach the age of retirement (the younger generations already know the pension is insolvent and aren't burdened by any such expectations). It's a recipe for change from within.

And what can we look forward to as the show winds down? Are you ready to see the economic landscape here littered with corpses and burning hulks? The BOJ has already rolled back quantitative easing, and the yen is looking stronger of late. But for the Prime Minister (and Shinzo Abe, his hand-picked successor) to keep pushing this disastrous two-pronged charge by government and business (which he deems his mandate based on the 2005 election results, despite the many voices in opposition), he's going to have to make up for it by restructuring elsewhere.

Let's take a step back here and make a frank appraisal of where Japan stands today. Confronted with an aging demographic and shrinking population, if we hope to achieve stability and autonomy in the future, we're going to need to change the employment system to allow for full participation by the young and old of both genders, and at the same time make a great leap forward in productivity. Conventional wisdom has it that the key to increasing productivity is workforce training, but to make a real go of it requires substantial increases in the variety of both businesses and jobs. The way the world works now, the rich are set up to exploit everyone at the mean and below, and they're quick to interfere when anyone tries to set up shop for themselves, preferring to keep everyone playing their game by their rules. That's why so many people get discouraged and opt out of the labor force. The key to breaking the exploitative stranglehold of the wealthy doesn't involve any need for a fight; the first step is to create more jobs and businesses that people really care about and want to work in. Step two is enabling more strategic job selection. A system needs to be in place to help people find work that suits and makes the most of their experience, their philosophy, their skill sets and abilities. The third factor is synergism. Productivity is usually talked about in terms of individual output, but synergies arise through the efforts of teams, and through internal teamwork and external collaborations with one's customers and on the regional and national scale, synergies that can be the key to dramatic boosts in productivity. Indeed, only by ramping up the synergistic effects of working together will it be possible to emerge stable and autonomous from the cutthroat competition of the modern world. A look around at the rest of the world reveals plenty of examples of countries that have given free market-style reforms the boot and managed to slip out from under the American umbrella. But while resource-rich places like Canada and Russia can afford to go it alone at least part of the way, I can't think of a case in which a country has been able to gain its autonomy by completely overhauling its economy.

The Koizumi-engineered squandering and sell-off of the country's wealth by turning the keys to national markets over to US interests, however, has meant nothing but injury and ignominy for Japan. Deregulation, privatization, the crowbarring open of markets and the enforcement of Darwinian law have reduced Japan's once wealthy and egalitarian, nearly classless, society to an American client state that is increasingly tethered in fiefdom to foreign interests; at the mercy of speculators, insiders and rigged tables; fractured by wider gaps between the rich and poor; and persuaded by domestic and international media alike that somehow the situation is of its own making. What needs to be remembered is that Japan is a goose that the farmer sees ripe for plucking.

When the US occupied Japan after the end of the Second World War, GHQ found itself presiding over a collection of cities of smoking rubble, a population disillusioned and fragmented after its total defeat, and a government past collapse. The initial efforts to support the rebuilding appeared benign, even idealistic, at first—a new constitution that guaranteed basic rights for all citizens and renounced war, and a democratization intended to ensure that militarist cabals would never be able to drape themselves in emperor worship again.

Then came war in Korea, and things changed quickly. The Dulles doctrine of containment and "liberation," ran into its first major stumbling block, and Japan, which had been serving as a kind of project in nation-rebuilding suddenly took on a new appeal as aircraft carrier and materiel depot parked conveniently off the coast of a major theater of conflict, and idealists found themselves being frog-marched out the door. Protests were squelched, war era bureaucrats and industry leaders were reinstated in power, and the population was mobilized in a drive to keep the GIs fighting in Pusan. It was during this turnaround that many of the institutions that characterize the government-industry-financial complex were thrown into action, propelled perhaps by the angular momentum. It was here that the nascent free press got neutered, banks fell into convoy formation, manufacturing took off, guaranteed lifetime employment became the corporate norm, domestic communism faded into irrelevance and the security pact with the States hardened into iron. Of course there were hiccoughs after the war ended and production was ramped back down, but the forces that had been set in motion continued to grow and evolve, and have prevailed ever since. A foreign-owned government divorced from the national interest and distanced from the global stage, the culture of conspicuous consumerism and manufactured consent, the tame media and the recent collective apathy, anomie and *Weltschmerz*—all trace back to the conflict in Korea (which, incidentally, is also where a certain neighboring country started entertaining ideas about lobbing rockets and manufacturing nukes).

Fast-forward forty years, and Japan is seen reaping the whirlwind it has sown. After a world-beating round of ram-charged energy and optimism in the 1970s and 80s, the wheels came off and the enterprise skidded crazily across bumpy ground. The waning years of the Showa reign and the whole of the Heisei thus far has been one long doldrums, with occasional episodes of vertigo and queasiness. The asset bubble that broke roundabout 1991, which should have been enough of a slap in the face to wake the deepest somnambulist, only made the administration and ministries hunker down and circle the wagons, hoping to wait till the storm passed. Little did they realize that this was an artificial weather front, engineered by forces outside the country and winked at by sleeper agents within.

After watching the precipitous rise of Japan, first in amusement, finally in alarm, foreign monetary policymakers, led by the US took measures to rectify the gaping trade deficit. (Back then trade imbalances were still considered serious by the United States, unlike at present, where they're seen as part of the natural order of things. America has since learned the unhealthy lesson that it can run up as large a national debt as it wants and no one will press it for payment. It's an economy based on the verity of the proposition that you can't go broke spending money you never had to begin with.) The Plaza Accord was entered into by the world's five leading economies in 1985—the US and Japan, plus the UK, France and West Germany—in which it was agreed take the greenback down a peg in order to yank the States out of a long recession and help restore its current account deficit to an acceptable level. That was all well and good for the US, but Japan, which recklessly allowed the yen to soar to double its pre-Plaza value over the following two years, found itself forced to market its goods overseas in outlandishly pricey currency.

The five years from 1986 to 1990 were heady ones while they lasted, characterized by all the excesses of an asset price bubble, with the Imperial Palace grounds famously worth more than all of California, and Japanese banks and conglomerates snapping up highly visible corporate prizes and trophy real estate with their seemingly bottomless trove of yen. Somewhere, though, a cadre of prescient insiders to the Accord must have been chuckling discreetly into their sleeves, knowing that their sucker had swallowed the bait. After all, hadn't they met not two years after their closed door session at the Plaza Hotel, this time to put an end to the dollar's plummet, stopping the yen's rise in its tracks and leaving the Japanese parvenus just enough golden braid to hang themselves with? One good tweak deserves another.

When the Tokyo stock and real estate markets finally woke up in 1999 as it became clear just how overpriced shares and land had become. The bubble collapsed gradually, almost apologetically, with none of the hysteria and social chaos that might normally be associated with the erasure of what amounted to 20 trillion dollars of national wealth. The Lost Decade set in with its mute stoicism and quiet desperation, and many foreign commentators came to call Japan's suffering invisible, even to question whether the country could truly be said to be suffering at all. Weren't the Japanese still among the world's most avid tourists and shoppers? Didn't Tokyo's Prada and Louis Vuitton outlets still boast the highest revenues of any location on earth?

But the suffering was and continues to be real. The UN Office for Economic Cooperation and Development released its most recent economic survey of Japan in July of 2006, and despite its seemingly rosy prognosis on the health of the country's economy as a unit, it contained grim statistics on where the slow and sucking tides of the Lost Decade have left us. Perhaps most striking for me was the revelation that Japan's Gini index is now higher than the world average. This index is a measure of the evenness of the distribution of a nation's wealth, in which lower numbers indicate greater equality. A Gini index of zero would indicate perfectly equitable distribution to all members of a society, while a Gini index of 100 would mean that one household commanded every bit of wealth in the land. Japan has always prided itself on its egalitarianism—it's almost a commonplace, invoked by academics, commentators and politicians alike—other countries may have vicious, yawning chasms separating the economic losers from the winners, but in Japan, everyone is supposed to enjoy the benefits of their membership in a fair and decent society. That is no longer the case. Japan's Gini index now sits at about 31, above the OECD average, putting it in the company of infamous have/have-not societies, such as the US and China, which both have indices near 40.

The number alone is a shocker, but the accompanying analysis makes for some extremely disturbing reading. The losses in socioeconomic parity are seen as the result of a mix of factors that run directly counter to the ideals shared by most Japanese. The tragedy here is that the people that need the most help and support from society—children, the elderly, single parents, the working poor—are left to fend for themselves. Poverty reduction receives short shrift from the government and now the cracks are beginning to show. By 2000, Japan's child poverty rate had risen to above the OECD mean, and a rapidly growing number of seniors is finding it harder and harder to make ends meet. The national budget is in sorry shape already after decades of boondoggles, LDP pork, taxpayer-financed bail-outs, and spendthrift public works, and now the prospect of wave after wave of retirees overwhelming the already buckling pension system, coupled with the downsizing of the Japanese population that began in earnest last year, means it's a bad time for those in need.

Perhaps the biggest factor at work here, though, has been the de-regularization of the workforce. The image of the salaryman, fiercely loyal to his firm and secure in the knowledge that his job is his job for life is quickly becoming a thing of the past. Graduation-to-grave job security was one of the hallmarks of the Japanese miracle, a system that was first introduced by companies eager to hold on to their staff and know-how when trained labor was at a premium and the economy was on a roll. But those articles of faith were called into doubt by a string of massive business closures from the mid-90s on, and even among the loyal lifers, there's a sense that the firm may not be the All-Provider it may once have seemed.

For many of the young, such faith and loyalty doesn't even figure into the equation. Rising numbers of freshly minted grads join the workforce as temps, contract employees or "freeters" (part-time, freelance or non-permanent staff). Many others join not at all, preferring the NEET (not in employment, education or training) way of life. Agnostic and non-committal, the young are in fact more attuned to the emptiness and insecurity of the current system than are their elders who dwell within its bowels. This is one thing that has never failed to impress me when I talk to people in their 20s and even teens; they sense intuitively that the old ways are rapidly fading and a new age is upon us. Although they may seem unmotivated or apathetic if measured by the 20th century yardstick, the truth is that they are already beginning to construct new networks and associations of people with shared values and beliefs. They see the way out and it lies in the future, not the past; the momentum is theirs.

That is not to say the path to a new 21st century way of life will be free and clear. There are powerful forces and vested interests arrayed to forestall the inevi-table. Which brings us back to Koizumi and his regime. What drives this admin-istration, what dark ambitions govern its dealings? The greed for power is certainly there, but that is no different from many governments in other times and lands. The key to understanding their mentality is that at heart they are afraid. After years of dog-eat-dog clawing and neck-biting, putting profit ahead of people and self ahead of all, they can see the tempest gathering on the horizon and know that all their money and status will be as nothing when the clouds finally break. The day is approaching when the game will shut down altogether, and the winnings that the bullies, liars and cheats have managed to amass will suddenly show their true value—wrinkled paper chits, shiny tokens and vacuous symbols of success, useful as garden compost or heating fuel, but perhaps a bit too rough for toilet paper.

Of course, while these trinkets and notions still hold some accepted value, the winners have a tremendous stake in ensuring not only that they keep right on winning, but that everybody else keeps playing their game. Because when the wheel finally stops spinning, wealth will be measured in friendships and social trust, and no number of chips or tokens will buy things of true value. Today, the winners include in Japan appear to be the ruling coalition, the corporate old guard and the new school of money-first capitalists. But they are by no means a unified front, victims of an intrinsic fractiousness that stands at the heart of the Winners vs. Losers mindset.

But what would cause Japan's own leaders to embrace what is at heart an alien creed? The roots of the Anglo-Saxon model are shallow here, but they found fertile ground in the wreckage after the War in the Pacific. Lest I be accused of historical revisionism, let me make it clear here that the war was Japan's great error and shame, the outcome of envy, fear and a crisis of confidence in its own native traditions and culture on the part of a powerful minority faction in the military and the ruling class. Certainly, the social and economic upheaval that preceded it contributed to the expansionist mood, and the enforced tendency to compromise and accept on the part of the people, which has such positive effects on social harmony in more peaceful times, also played a major role. And when that witless adventure brought about total defeat, perhaps it was inevitable that the ensuing vacuum would be filled by whatever alternative presented itself first, which in the event was none other the then-triumphant Anglo-American way.

The Occupation forces found themselves confronted with a much less hostile and much more accommodating population than they had prepared themselves for, and soon began reinstalling powerful bureaucrats business leaders and political factions into seats of power, as the most immediately effective means of rebuilding the fallen nation. The reinstated, who were immediately deputized to carry out all kinds of American agendas from fighting communism to launching a client state, economy and financial system, almost certainly felt relief and gratitude in equal measure, for the confused and arbitrary war crime tribunal had painted a grim scenario of the prospects for wartime leaders. But more importantly, the power, perks and possibilities that opened up after the departing GHQ handed back the keys to the country provided a powerful object lesson in the value of cooperating with the powerful, without qualm, that has endured among the ruling elite right up to the present day. Now, as then, the United States is the world's superpower and therein lies the key to deciphering Koizumi, Abe, the LDP and their cronies in the upper crust. It is another kind of collaboration, more akin to the Vichy in league with the Germans, which has guided them to lead the country so far down this perilous path.

When Market Theory Fails

The economic world of the 20th century was defined by a group of academics who shared what has been collectively termed as a neo-classical approach. In this view, economics is the set of activities by agents who reliably act with perfect rationality and full and equal access to information to maximize their economic benefit (or, "utility"). These rational, omniscient agents quickly arrive at a state of divine equilibrium in which each reaps the optimum reward. That's how it works on paper, anyway. But even proponents of the neoclassical model acknowledge it is at best a poor reflection of the actual way people conduct their business and make transactions, relying on statistics to smooth out the plentiful outliers and exceptions, and much recent work in economics has served to overturn the model in its entirety. Economic science is proving now what has always been plain—that people don't always act rationally, that not everyone has the same amount or quality of information, and that as a consequence markets are perennially in disequilibrium. Just as physics and math were forced to confront their bugbears by demonstrations of relativity, quantum uncertainty and incompleteness, old-school economics has had to answer its critics.

The problem is, many of the architects of current-day systems were schooled in the neoclassical mode, and even those who were not have a strong vested interest in ensuring that the scheme appears to work fairly, and not in the arbitrary, opaque and asymmetric way that it actually does. With the final abandonment of the gold standard last century, the world came to accept and recognize (although we often forget) that money—stamped into metal, printed on paper or simply floating in the ether as electronic data—has value independent of any commodity. Money is information. And, remarkably, the converse of that is equally true: information is money. More specifically, the control of information is now the surest means to the acquisition of wealth, and the only means to maintain it.

This situation enables a vicious pattern of wealth consolidation through reality management in the form of market manipulation. The details are arduous, dense and beyond the scope of this book, but we can synopsize them as follows before moving on to the near-term consequences. What we have now is a new riff on the fundamental mechanism that underlies the whole principle of capital wealth: a person or group of people develops a means of stockpiling value, and leverages the surplus into accumulating even more—a kind of snowball effect. In the improbable logic of classical economics, the actions of multiple agents all working in their own enlightened self-interest ensures that the system tends to a happy medium in which everyone is doing what he or she does best and participating in the system on more or less equal footing. But history and common sense argue otherwise. In the earliest economies it may have been simply that the physically stronger came to predominate and command an inordinate share of wealth, and soon it was those with the best technology in arms and fortification that came to rule fiefs and kingdoms. Equilibrium was kept only by the maintenance of standing armies and strategic forts, an uneasy peace that could erupt into war at the slightest prompting.

But as civilization and the rule of law established themselves as the new norm, resort to arms was increasingly seen as crude, barbaric and, more importantly, uneconomical. But as the empowered remained unwilling to relinquish their advantage, an alternative to violence had to be formulated, which led in a relatively short time to the secular practice of information control (although it should be acknowledged that the consolidation of power through selective suppression of information has been employed by theocracies throughout history).

So just as von Clausewitz called war "the continuation of policy by other means," now the control of information might be called the continuation of conflict by other means. The asymmetry of access to reliable information is the most effective stratagem ever developed of controlling populations. This can take many forms, from the simple refusal to share information that might have value, to more sophisticated tactics involving media spin, perception management and the manufacture of consent, and the blacker arts of propaganda, psychological operations and the sponsored promulgation of falsehoods.

Deception is an old game, to be sure, but where it once was the province of state and church, now we find it pervades the market economy. The entire market mechanism, although ostensibly built as a level field for transactions between generally equal players, is in fact a fabulously biased faith-based system founded entirely on misplaced trust. This has been true since the earliest economic bubbles, all the way back to Dutch tulipomania in the mid-1600s, John Law's visionary scheming (France) and the South Seas crash (England) of the early 18th century, through every other rigged game, pyramid sales or Ponzi scheme, the market failure that led to the Great Depression, and the predictable spate of national economic blowouts in Britain (70s), the US (80s) and Japan (90s), not to mention the gargantuan corporate and trading swindles we've been treated to several times a decade for the past 25 years.

The details vary but the underlying mechanism is always fundamentally the same: some trusted clerisy, generally the high priests of the financial sector, is entrusted with discretionary access to huge amounts of capital solely on the strength of their promise to create more wealth from it for their flocks. They make the same fantastic promises to more and more people, and the situation becomes more and more untenable until finally the bubble inflated with all of those collective hopes, reckless dreams and wishful investments bursts, canceling out enormous wealth, simply wiped off the ledgers in the insolvency proceedings that ensue. Of course, with the exception of a sacrificial lamb or two, the majority of the high priests, who could see the bubble for what it was from the beginning, walk away not merely unscathed, but enriched, from the fire sale bargains and short-selling opportunities that became available as reality dawned and panic set in.

For the ordinary person (which means anyone without access to financial industry shop-knowledge), the end of a bubble spells disaster. But—and this is a very big but—for the privileged insiders, bubbles are beautiful engines of wealth, both on the way up and as they come crashing down. This is not always apparent when you read the financial pages after a market crash. The stories of doom and glom generally suggest that everyone got burned and that no one came out a winner. It would be naïve folly to believe so, although certainly the winners are happy not to have their ugly profiteering brought to light. And so they pay to whitewash and conceal the truth, turning a portion of their gains to the strategic manipulation of public consciousness by the media. And so the circle turns once again—asymmetry of information creates bubbles based on what Alan Greenspan liked to call "irrational exuberance," leading to massive profit-taking by tiny informed minorities at the cost of even more massive losses by the benighted majority, followed by a new round of dissimulation, denial and deception in the aftermath even as the next bubble (junk bonds, Tokyo real estate, dot coms, hedge funds, REITs, whatever) begins to swell to life.

In recent years the system has become even more efficient as the moneyed and the powerful take advantage of information technology and media control to paint pictures and send targeted messages to ever-wider audiences. A report on CNN or a major newswire is guaranteed to circle the world within minutes, and carry the evangelical weight of scripture revealed, with the power to impact markets instantaneously and profoundly. The ability to sway the supposedly neutral media is one of the greatest assets—indeed, it may be the trump card—held by big money. Remember, the ability to influence news can create great value even when reports fail to agree with reality. The news creates reality. If a prominent spokesman or pundit furrows his brow at oil prices, interest rates or the yuan-dollar exchange rate, markets sensitive to those factors immediately begin to fibrillate. If a report, even an groundless rumor, airs on a major network or financial news service that Amalgamated Corn Silk's forthcoming quarterly seems likely to disappoint, then you can be sure its stock will plummet in real-time. Just like that, bits of electronic data of one variety (news information) affect other bits of another (stock prices). Media control is an incredibly valuable asset.

Of course, the appearance of neutrality is part of the maintenance of that value, and so no little effort goes into maintaining that pretense. Lack of trust in the media leads to simmering civil dissent like we're seeing in China, where readers say of *The People's Daily* that the only item in the paper you can trust is the date. But now the advent of new media—blogs, vlogs, podcasts, eyewitness digital photography and video, alternative news sources, and unsponsored and uncensored commentary, have caused the veil of objective media begin to fray. And once that tidal wave of fresh views and objective (or at least not overtly manipulated) accounts breaks and highlights the perjured news we've been subject to, then the real fun will start—an epiphany that will disabuse the world of its unjustified faith in a system that has been a fixed game from day one.

Some years ago, I worked in the field of econometrics. Economic data is by nature incomplete, so no matter how we refined our analytical methods, the results were necessarily imperfect. Mathematical analyses of finance suffer from similar uncertainties, with price manipulations and market distortion by oligopolies and monopolies and making it impossible to derive accurate analytical results. And when even the media themselves are subject to spin and manipulation, the situation arises in which the sole means of knowing the truth is directly through one's own senses. I've read widely and had many different experiences, but I have to admit that my real feeling is that the only way to arrive at the truth is through approaching the world by honing one's natural clarity of mind. And I believe that more and more people are coming to terms with the limitations of knowledge, the epistemological limits of neoclassical economics, and are now seeking to restore the balance between that which is known with that which can only be felt.

Currency, stock values, land prices, and all the exotic instruments of financial alchemy—it's a faith-based economy we live in, equal parts voodoo and legerdemain. And faith is the key, the belief that even if hard work is a sucker's game, at least there's still hope for the lucky, the gambler's false conviction that while the wheel may be capricious, the odds are the same for all. Without that willingness to believe, the whole show crumbles and people pull their money back out of investments to safer havens—stuffing their mattresses with it if need be. Without a certain assurance of faith, who would plunk down cash on speculation? The system has a strong interest in maintaining that notion that even if the odds are long, they're just as long for everyone. Faith (and with it, hope) is the key.

The day is coming soon when hope for the old ways will be lost—in fact, I would argue that that day has already passed, although unnoticed by many. But that does not mean the death of hope itself. Rather, we are now witnessing the birth of a new system, one not twisted by a let-them-eat-cake sense of noblesse, encumbered with pernicious legacies, tortured by Darwinian ethics or corrupted with raw greed. This is Japan's forlorn hope, a lassitude and defeatism that has characterized the Heisei Era thus far. We're already six years into the 21st century. People are much more aware than they were even in the Showa days, and are working toward and expecting to be able to lead Lifestyles of Health and Sustainability.

As just a single example of a pervasive problem, the Aneha building scandal in late 2005 (in which an architectural design firm deliberately falsified earthquake resistance data as a cost-cutting measure) ran smack in the face of everything LOHAS stands for and exceeded the public's already strained capacity for forgiveness. Of all the purchases in one's lifetime, buying a home is one of the largest and expected to be one of the longest-lasting. To have those expectations dashed by fraudulent building plans or shoddy construction is simply intolerable. The wheedling and transparently self-serving excuses of the builders, developers and inspectors on the Diet floor seem like a shameless taunt to the LOHAS congregation. The old Showa rationales of, "That's just how business works," and, "You get what you pay for," can longer stand unchallenged.

Such are the symptoms of an even larger problem, what has been referred to as the sociopathic nature of the corporation. A look at the history of organized business reveals a very enlightening evolution of legislation, born in America, that transformed corporations from transient, purpose-specific entities to the long-lived and dominant all-pervasive transnational forces they have become. The history of the ascendancy of major corporations to positions of power rivaling those of national governments (without being subject to as many checks and balances or other regulatory niceties) is an interesting one, although at times it can be uncomfortable to ponder, for the end result of the strained interpretation of the 14th Amendment to the US Constitution is that corporations are legal entities with a full slate of human rights (including the rights to life, liberty and the pursuit of happiness) without any of the constraints of conscience or responsibility.

Personhood without humanity. And the success of that model was quickly exported around the world, a super-efficient meme that steamrolled or gobbled up any attempts to cut it off or rein in its proliferation. Global corporations now command the world's wealth, workforces and culture to a depth and extent that is the envy of the most ambitious politician, and in an entirely undemocratic, unrepresentative way. But more importantly, corporations, which after all are soulless organizations, have tended over time to bypass or evolve away from any moral constraint on their ability to maximize profit. The single motivation of the corporation is black ink on the bottom line—and the implications and actual impacts of that have been profound.

In this new century, however, people are placing a priority on a sense of right and wrong, and amoral firms no longer hold a carte blanche. In the 21st century, it's accepted that things of quality command a higher price. It's an age in which, if you don't have the money to pay for something today, you save so that you can buy it tomorrow. And it's an age in which organizations are emerging that will enable and encourage each person to fulfill their own potential without needless stress or worry. People will determine for themselves what constitutes a life of health and sustainability in line with their own preferences and limitations, and horizontal leadership will step up to steer the networks that will frame the life-styles of the day. This is no idealized vision of a future utopia, it's starting to happen in the here and now, with the ranks of the like-minded growing every day. And neither is this some dilettantism of the rich; many Japanese of every walk of life and income class are waking up to this way of thinking. For the succession of lapdog administrations and their designs on an Anglo-Saxon revolution, that is sure to spell the end.

This age of reform needs to escape both from superannuated Showa Era practices and the ultra-competitive Heisei mindset. When I speak with today's college students, rough in manners and appearance though they may be, it's as if they've already left behind those mired in the old Showa and Heisei ways, and are much more aware and alive to the synergistic benefits of teamwork, the importance of setting goals, the drive toward progress and a better world and affinity for the LOHAS ideal. Japan is now going through the process of shedding those mired in outdated value system, as witnessed by the spate of recent troubles and incidents, but once these transitional pains have subsided, I feel we are set to move into a grand and glorious new era of growth and prosperity.

There is hope for corporations as well. As entities, corporations are limited only by the direction, or lack thereof, they receive from people; they cannot think for themselves. Perversely, it is now common to say that people work for corporations, when it is the corporations that are supposed to be working for us. But now, a new generation of ethically minded and optimistic young entrepreneurs is seizing opportunity where it presents itself to break out from the constraints of the old establishment and launch new companies on their own terms. Here in Japan, we've seen the recent passage of a new corporation law that bypasses existing commercial laws involving minimum capital requirements, making it impossible to start a new limited company (*yuugen kaisha*), while at the same time making it much easier to fully incorporate (*kabushiki kaisha*); new rules that mean that anyone will be able to start his or her own business. As more and more people are looking to get out of big corporations and work for themselves or launch a startup, the Japanese economy will become increasingly network- and teamwork-intensive. Big projects will be undertaken by collaboratives of small firms working together, and as different philosophies and value sets bring diversity to the network and reconfigure the entire economy on value lines, we're going to see a growth of the Japanese economy that will be heaven to some and hell to others. In the days ahead, whom you know will be more important than what you earn or own. That this was made possible by the US-authored wave of domestic market deregulation, intended to bring Japan's wealth even closer within reach of global capital makes it all the more delicious. The moral of the story: ingenuity triumphs over avarice. Just one more cause for hope.

I often write about the "winners" and "losers" to describe those who prevail over and those who get buried by their times. Someone who exploits the weak to enrich himself might appear to be a winner, but in actuality, since the current state of the world cannot endure, in the end such a person is only a victimizer of others and a victim of the times. These days, with the climate of industry and finance such as it is, any notion of winning or losing has become effectively meaningless—only those who look to take care of their customers, to work for the real betterment of the world, can be called winners. But few people realize that, and the vast majority of the older generations are still trapped in the dog-eat-dog mindset. It's an ethic that says, "Keep telling the big lie right up to the end, and if you get caught, disappear." It tells you, "You're at war with your neighbors. Do whatever it takes to win." A world where this is the social norm is a world gone crazily awry, and it should come as no surprise when we see events like the recent savageries committed by those who have lapsed into despair or simply split from reality altogether.

The management of the rogues' gallery of firms implicated in recent scandals and cover-ups in Japan may have all confessed to the charges against them, but I can only laugh when I see them indicted as criminals by po-faced commentators.

We're still in an overall deflationary economy, only a handful of firms or individuals are making any money, and real estate prices are staying down. But don't the banks still finance peoples and companies with that same real estate as collateral? Don't banker paychecks remain fat? Does anyone seriously believe that lenders could continue to report profits without resorting to duplicitous or at least irresponsibly creative accounting practices? The illicit paper-shuffling at UFJ, the internal whistleblower warnings at the Hamaoka and Fukushima nuclear plants, the surreptitious recalls by Mitsubishi, the self-bred troubles at Daiei and Kokudo—what's the difference with these? Broad swathes of any industry sector are now propped up on crutches or foundations of lies. They'd collapse if the truth were to be aired. Even if specific evidence of this yet has yet to be brought out into the light, all of us can feel it in our bones.

The problem isn't limited to the executive ranks; it involves every employee, even their families, in a web of cover-ups and blind-eyed avoidance. Is it any wonder there's no audience for the truth? People can no longer face the truth, or even conceive of taking the lead in bringing about a change. A proactive approach to change has been supplanted by a see, hear and speak no evil attitudinal blindness and passive acceptance, even as opportunities for change pass by. But loans need to be serviced, kids sent to college and appearances maintained, so everyone's willing to keep up the secret for the sake of their monthly paycheck. It's not exactly a ski jump into the void, but everyone's hanging out there, toes over the edge, keeping up the façade of lies, pushing ugly troubles out of sight, holding out, day after day, forestalling the inevitable landing (or crash).

Much has been written about what distinguishes leaders from managers. It's been said many times before, and remains true: Managers do what's right, leaders decide what's right. In this day and age, the leaders have decided it's right to conceal and prevaricate, and the rank and file management is busy working to execute that game plan. Organizations don't need more managers, they need more leaders; leaders to right our errant course. When the Indian Ocean tsunami struck in 2004, it terrified people who'd been trying to set themselves apart from nature. The same kind of catastrophe is gathering force here in Japan. Some here believe that we're surrounded by threats, people immune to reason, the dangerous and the simply unpleasant—some people just hope to avoid and ignore them. But when events like the recent horrors in the news take place, these same people lose fall into despair. People who fell like they're beset by a hostile world can't help but succumb to a siege mentality, fear piled on fear, until they collapse under the strain.

But there is a simple route out of this Slough of Despond: seek out and work to achieve ways of living together with others. Live in concert, not in conflict, with Nature. The world is a world of diversity. If society provides the systems to enable man and his environment to fulfill their natural roles, people will flourish and live in peace. That's how we've been designed from the beginning to realize our true potential and perform at peak levels. I've said it before—if we want to make a Japan that people will want to visit, if we hope to rebuild our economy from the ground up on the individual and the national scale, we need to find real-world workable solutions to allow people to coexist with Nature and thrive, to root out entrenched prejudice and ill will, to create an economy where it's possible for families to live happily together freed from the need to lie, and to allow people the time they need to discover their true callings in life. It's a philosophy of providing opportunities for people in every field of endeavor to undertake new challenges.

The Threat to the Biosphere

With all the troubles besetting modern man and modern societies, it is easy to lose sight of the big picture, which, for the sake of convenience, let's call Life on Earth. Life on Earth has had its ups and downs over the past four billion years—the big move from anaerobic to aerobic metabolism, the why-the-hell-not experimentalism of the Cambrian Explosion, volcanoes, giant meteorites, Ice Ages and floods—Life has seen it all. But now there's this one tiny, seemingly insignificant branch of the phylogenetic tree, naked apes with plenty of forebrain and some big ideas, that looks ready to start modifying the rules that have seen life through it's first few eons. It's a brain just big enough to ask the boldest questions …

"Do we need nature?" It's a question that can only be rhetorical. Imagine for a moment a person who answered in the negative. Such a response could only be either intentionally argumentative or based on a strained interpretation of the terms ("What exactly do you mean when you say 'nature'?" "Just who is this 'we,' anyway?"). Most of us, however, will acknowledge our debt to and dependence on nature. We are all avid and regular consumers of natural food, water and air, and it is difficult to conceive how we'd get along without them. Our bodies and minds and, indeed, the fundamental stuff of matter, energy, time and space all seem to be natural in a very basic way. Once we have granted to nature that purview, the question of its necessity can effectively be considered moot. We do need nature; it would be ridiculous to conclude otherwise. But in reaching that conclusion, it seems only natural for us to ask, "Yes we need nature, but can we, (or do we need to), do any better?"

The urge to improve on nature is located deep in the core of the human psyche. Nature has given us life. She is, in a broad sense our mother, provider of all things that make our existence. But she is mother also to bee stings and tooth decay, to diseases and storms, to famine, drought and freezing cold. Nature engenders life and joy, but also pain and death. It is here that the camps are divided and the battle lines drawn in the debate over just how much natural discomfort we ought to be prepared to live with as part of our inheritance, and how much we should attempt to change. Because it seems that now we humans have

31

become a force of nature, capable of altering our environment on a scale that in the past was reserved to such telluric, astronomical or evolutionary events: volcanism, meteoritic impacts, the advent of anaerobic bacteria, and the rise of life from the sea. Scientists have gone so far as to propose a new geological epoch, the Anthropocene, in acknowledgement of the planet-wide consequences of human technology, population growth and diaspora. It should be noted that this is not a term for a hypothetical future age—the Anthropocene began three centuries ago. Humanity has changed the face of the earth, has irrevocably altered the biosphere, and our power to do so increases every day. But while the record of our past activities is clear, the outcome remains in question.

Stewart Brand famously suggested, "Since we are gods, we might as well get good at it." There are those who would say we're good at it already. While humanity has by no means managed to build itself a universal paradise, a significant percentage of the population lives longer, healthier and more prosperously than any previous generation. And while the great majority of mankind does not enjoy the unprecedented material prosperity characteristic of life in a developed nation, our overall success as a species is attested to by our exponential population growth and our dominion over every inhabitable corner of the world. We sit alone at the top of the food chain, and have yoked nature to our needs and wants. If we can eat it, burn it, build with it, or even just put it on a shelf and admire it, we probably already have.

But none of this is new. Humans have been the most successful large animal species on earth since pre-historic times. In evolutionary terms, the combination of thumbs, voice boxes and big brains is a winning adaptation. What is new, however, is the payoff of that evolution: technology. What began as a trickle with fire, tool use and agriculture has now become a flood, a rushing cataract that only shows signs of increasing in intensity. And this is where the burden of our deity becomes clear. Our ascent was dictated by natural selection, a plodding, gradual process when viewed at the human scale. But our capacity for invention and foresight is now letting us leap in knight's moves over many of the traditional constraints.

The big science stories of the last century were nuclear energy, space travel and information technology—forces with the potential to alter the evolutionary playing field or perhaps to end the game entirely. Bio- and nano-technology promise even greater, even more ominous discoveries. It is reasonable (but nonetheless surprising) to expect that we will be able to change the very nature of nature within the lifetime of the current generation. What is more disconcerting is that the pace of progress is now so fast that we can't even predict with confidence what the next big thing might be, much less how it will change the world when it arrives.

The mind staggers, not just at the prospects, but at the lack of sufficient information with which to form a satisfyingly clear mental picture of what the future might hold. In reaching our present summit, we've found that the horizons stretch infinitely in all directions and watch in awe and consternation as the effects of our actions in any part of that realm ripple across both space and time and quickly pass out of our range of vision. We tinker with nature incessantly, we even have the means to give it a mighty shove, but we can't really tell if it's going to shatter to pieces, shove back, or just obligingly let itself be moved.

Few things are less instructive than a discussion in which none of the participants has all of the information they need to build a case. This does not, however, prevent us from having them. The perennial debate between the champions of technological progress and the advocates of restraint is characterized by precisely such a deficit, which might be merely entertaining if not for the severity of the potential consequences. On the one hand, the Full Speed Ahead team tells us we're doing fine, that things just keep getting better in a Panglossian way. Or they play the fear card and say that we have to keep running just to prevent being left by the wayside in a Red Queen's race where the losing side goes extinct.

The other side of the debate calls for an immediate and forceful application of the brakes. Evolutionarily, environmentally and ethically, our works have gotten out of our control and we need to take an immediate time out, if not to reverse the damage, at least to catch our collective breath and take a clear-eyed look at just what it is we've wrought. Both teams can call on deep benches of impeccably credentialed scientists, renowned authorities and other conscientious and thoroughgoing thinkers to support their views. If we allow that all sides of the discussion are arguing in good faith (the alternative is to accuse one or more of the principals of willfully seeking to limit human quality of life or even to bring about our extinction, which requires a more pessimistic view of human nature than I care to espouse), then it becomes clear that the debate is really a question of confidence versus caution. Some would say hubris versus fear. But at the end of the day, the general truth underlying every case is that we just don't know what lies ahead. We don't have that data.

Uncertainty is not unnatural. In fact, the reverse is true. As Voltaire noted, "Doubt is uncomfortable, but certainty is absurd." We have evolved amid such uncertainty to the extent that now we are simultaneously becoming able to appreciate just how precarious and contingent our stance is, and to have the power to take a conscious and active role in shaping our world. We can mold and harness the environment, we can rewrite genes, we can build molecules to order and make atoms explode. We can do all these things and more, but we can never really be sure of where those paths will lead. And perhaps that is what will keep us honest as we play this game whose rulebook we find is now ours to edit.

We have taken for ourselves tremendous powers and by corollary, tremendous responsibility. Unfortunately, mankind's record in the modern era has been less than exemplary. Given the choice between instant gratification at the cost of environmental devastation and slower, more earth-friendly practices, humans as a species have consistently opted for the former. But the dividend of that short-sightedness has already begun to catch up with us. Pollution, greenhouse warming, disastrous losses of biodiversity and depletion of natural resources, environmental uglification and a generalized squandering of nature's bounty are among the greatest problems to confront mankind and they are all of our own making. And even more than the structural defects inherent in the world's economic and financial systems today, these environmental crises represent true threats to humanity's continued survival. The very concept of economic activity, as a function of living agents (people) is necessarily subsumed in larger questions about how life itself can be sustained.

Japan has played its part in these anthropogenic crises, from the manufacturing boom that contaminated water and land with dioxin, asbestos and PCBs, to the massive boondoggle spending on rural development that ripped up, raped and paved over much of the country's natural beauty, to the imported consumerist aesthetic that encourages constant, conspicuous consumption without a fig for the consequences. But we are beginning to awaken to the dangers and to take steps to remedy our mistakes.

Of leading nations, Japan stands somewhere about midway between the enlightened and the offenders. Its support of initiatives such as the Kyoto Protocol, recycling and the development of hybrid cars and biodegradable materials has been admirable, but its culture of conspicuous consumption, emphasis on disposable novelties and trend fashions that change in an eye-blink have been less worthy of praise. What I would argues is that, soon, there will be no option to persist in these unsustainable habits as the natural resources that make them possible are dwindling to the point of extinction.

The biosphere is at risk on nearly every front imaginable. Mass extinctions, climate change, rapine exploitation—Mother Nature has had a bad 150 years since the start of the industrial revolution. Of all the looming crises, Peak Oil appears to be the wave that will break on humanity first. Imagine a world in which gasoline costs ten times what it costs today (in real, not inflation-adjusted terms). Imagine a world in which cars and trucks do not run, airplanes are grounded, plastics cannot be made and modern agriculture is starved of its omnipresent pesticides and petrochemical fertilizer. When the oil runs out (which even the most optimistic estimates figure will be sometime before 2050), we're looking at a world not very different from the Edo period in terms of the available transport and farming technologies. Say hello again to rail, sail, wagon and foot. More frighteningly though is the estimate that the best estimates of sustainable global population in a preindustrial world suggest one billion humans as a nice round number. If you're a bit uncomfortable thinking about what will become of the other five billion-plus souls now living or waiting to be born into a world system that has suddenly run out of gas, you should be.

Climate change, whether it's a manmade event or just another part of Heaven's scenario, is also gearing up to put man back in his place. The trends all head in the direction of continued global warming in the near term. Whether that trend will continue with all the attendant fallout—coastal flooding, desertification, heat islands, habitat loss and various greenhouse havoc—or whether it will reverse itself as a kind of first act to a new Ice Age, remain to be seen. They say everybody talks about the weather, but nobody ever does anything about it, and they're right. Nobody can. Whether the climate turns to fire or ice, it seems we have little choice in the matter at this point.

It would be nice to think that at least we won't be alone for the spectacle, but the patterns of species depletion suggest that the world will be a lonelier place, from a biodiversity perspective anyway. Scientists who study the earth's flora and fauna uniformly report that species are becoming extinct at the rapidest rate since the age of the dinosaurs. Tyrannosaurus at least had a gargantuan meteor to blame for its demise—a fitting, almost Wagnerian, end. These days, the environmental devastation is wrought by modern man's demand for fast food, cheap gas and plastic everything. How's that for an epitaph?

Science and technology have brought much good—longer life spans, lower infant mortality, less starvation, more mobility—to the human world, but a debt has been accruing. To the extent possible, we have asked other species to pay it on our behalf; after all, what's 10,000 acres of rainforest, more or less, weighed against our demand for pasturage for factory farmed beef? What's one species of butterfly? But now, we (some of us) are beginning to see, and call attention to the downsides. Do we really need genetically engineered radishes or blue roses? Are three incremental tweaks to plasma display technology really necessary every year?

Won't Nature do? I'd say that like it or not, in the next few decades (maybe sooner), we're about to find out. When ecology and economy collide, I don't think I need to tell you which has first claim to right of way. Man's aspirations have always featured a balance of the artificial with the natural, man's creations set in the context of Creation itself. But in the past few thousand years (an evolutionary eyeblink), the pendulum has swung drastically, up about as high as it can be expected to swing. The only direction left to go is down, and I think we're in for a wild and disorienting ride; it's a long way down, but we're dropping fast. Brace for impact.

Late Medieval Europe experienced famines caused by drastic amounts of rainfall, and the spread of infectious diseases such as the plague ultimately led to an overall reduction in the human population in that part of the world. The period also saw the start of the protracted and terrible Hundred Years' War between England and France. Now too, I feel that Europe and America have started to view their future with deep trepidation. The panics engendered by the Y2K bug and the 911 attacks have now deepened to an even grimmer ineffable dread. I suspect that climate upheavals are only the beginning of this year's world-changing events; it may be a year in which the West undergoes changes we might now think unimaginable. This may in fact be the year that people of the Western world will have cause to experience firsthand the *Weltanschauung* described by Johan Huizinga in his The Waning of the Middle Ages, or to reflect on the message of the Latin admonition, *Memento mori* ("Remember that thou must die").

The Birth of a New Japan

As we have seen, the first great postwar bubble came to Japan thanks to its good fortune of being the only developed nation of the second half of the 20th century in a position not to squander huge swathes of its national budget on defense spending and channel its energies exclusively into its economy. The downside of that was that Japan was also the first to experience a total bubble collapse. Now, more than a decade later, Europe and North America are primed to undergo the same. The principal cause of the Japanese asset bubble was the massive accumulation of corporate profits in the 1980s, compliments of the trade surplus that Japan was able to achieve thanks to the quality and volume of its manufacturing sector, which itself was a testament to Japan's meteoric revival. But, as we have also discussed, the great revival of post-war Japan was the result of the plans set in motion by the leaders of both the victors and the defeated. This did not occur in a vacuum; Japan's economic miracle was the joint product of domestic industriousness and the world's sanction.

When the Showa Emperor made his speech acknowledging defeat in the Pacific War, he said that Japan's task in the post-war period would be to "keep pace with the progress of the world." Add to this the allowance in the Potsdam Declaration that "Japanese participation in world trade relations shall be permitted" upon surrender, and we have a clear message to the Japanese people: though you may have been defeated in the military conflict, in the coming economic war, failure is not an option. The vision of the future handed down to Japan by the leaders of both countries at the end of the war was one in which Japan took a dominant position in world trade. And Japan, like an apt and eager pupil, adhered to this guiding vision diligently right up to the end of the Showa era (which lasted from 1926-1989), establishing itself as an economic leader and, by virtue of its trade surplus, becoming one of the world's richest nations.

As the 1980s drew to a close, Japan was awash in goods and money, and boasted a diamond-shaped demographic with a large middle class, assured public safety and no sign of (or true capability for) military aggression. Judged by these standards, Japan had become the most advanced nation in the world. Heisei Japan, however, suffers from a lack of a new vision capable of inspiring the people and informing their activities. It seems all we are left with is a vague nostalgia for the Showa good old days, and the sense that we should somehow seek a return to the way things were then. We have yet to receive a vision from the Japanese government or from abroad regarding the future of Japan with as much concrete direction as the decisions made at the end of World War II, something the Japanese people can feel in their hearts, something that creates a flow towards progress.

This lack of a unifying new vision is the primary cause of the pain felt throughout Japan today. In thinking of a future Japan, we cannot use Europe, America or other countries in Asia as models. Japan is unique in that no other nation in the world has achieved such great material wealth, safety and security for such a large percentage of its citizens. It was also the first nation to suffer a bubble collapse severe enough to shake the foundations of its entire economy. For better or worse, Japan continues to be at the leading edge.

Japan has always been quick to adopt new ideas and cultural elements, and has possessed a certain flexibility in the face of change. Japan has only been brought to its knees now, in the Heisei era, due to the lack of a new vision to replace that of the Showa period. We have no clear vision of the future, so we worry about losing what fleeting happiness and security we have now. To our great detriment, we have come to fear change.

Why can we not envision our future, even as it looms before us? Why has Japan's revival stalled? It is because we look overseas for models and answers instead of to our own people, land and history. Japan's worries are ours *because* we are so far ahead of the game. The world outside holds no answers to our dilemma. In the absence of vision, limitless self-interest (competition and greed) has become the foundation of our society, leaving few people truly inspired to do good. It took more than a decade after the beginning of the Heisei era before the majority of Japanese truly felt that we had crossed the first pass on the road to economic recovery.

What we really need to reshape now is the very conceptual basis of Japan itself, as a nation, not a mere political entity. By comparison, current issues such as government administration and elections, constitutional details, or the Imperial system are minor. When I say Japan, I refer to the conceptual whole that is imagined when people, both Japanese and non-Japanese, in the past, present, and future, mean or meant by the word. Confusion on this point is what has led to the parlous delay in Japan's reconstruction.

Now we need the kind of transformational vision into which the majority of Japanese can pour their hearts, their talents and energies. A vision does not mean a detailed blueprint, logical plan, or a tally of costs and benefits. It is a picture of oneself and one's society in the future that is felt in the heart and the gut. If we succeed in developing and carrying out that vision, we will serve as a model of success for other nations in Europe, North America, and Asia, who are walking a very similar path to our own. The rethinking of Japan may very plausibly trigger a reshaping of the world.

Looking outside, the U.S. ultimately failed in the attempt to restore its competitiveness, and so they have resorted to ploys and desperate tactics to generate fictitious capital on a grand scale. This fictive wealth was to be their portal to continued future prosperity and dominance. But the illusion soon collapsed due to its failure to jibe with reality, taking the silicon bubble it created down with it a few years back. Now, the impending demise of figmentary wealth itself has destabilized the real economy, which threatens an even larger collapse. The real problem here is that the fiction is uncontained—it has co-opted capital from all over the world, and the entire global economy finds itself teetering on the brink of disaster.

As global capital market strategist Hideaki Sonoyama noted in his November 29, 1995 article "The Pitfall of the Global Capital Market System (No. 5)," the United States took a lesson from the Great Depression that began with the stock market crash of 1929 and established three laws as a foundation for a new capital market system. He made some very astute analyses of one of those laws, the Securities Exchange Act of 1934, Section 2, in his "An Investigation into the Causes of the Great Depression … The Deficiencies of the Market System," which highlights all of the deficiencies of the trade economy system that led to the Great Depression, and I'd like to cite some of the more salient and telling items on this long but trenchant list:

> … prices of securities on such exchanges and markets are frequently susceptible to manipulation and control, and the dissemination of such prices gives rise to excessive speculation, resulting in sudden and unreasonable fluctuations in the prices of securities … [which] prevents a fair calculation of taxes … [and] the fair valuation of collateral for bank loans.… [a situation producing] widespread unemployment and the dislocation of trade, transportation, and industry.… National emergencies … are precipitated, intensified, and prolonged by manipulation and sudden and unreasonable fluctuations of security prices and by excessive speculation on such exchanges and markets …

> … to meet such emergencies the Federal Government is put to such great expense as to burden the national credit.

In essence, the cause of the Great Depression can be found in irregular fluctuations in the price of securities. That these securities' prices fluctuate and are susceptible to arrant speculation and unregulated manipulation is the main factor leading to chaos and collapse under the present financial regime. These sucker's game price fluctuations cause alternating unreasonable expansions and contractions of the credit volume and hinder the fair reckoning of taxes and valuation of collateral for bank loans, leading not only to the disruption of financial systems such as domestic markets and public finance, but also widespread unemployment and the disruption of the actual economy, downturns in manufacturing, you name it. Double plus ungood. The process of rebuilding from such a crash places a tremendous financial burden on the entire country, i.e. the taxpayers. (i.e., you and me.)

The reasons for the Great Depression as set forth in America's own Securities Exchange Act, and the chaos that followed that depression bear striking resemblance to what went down in Japan 60 years later. The chaos in the market economy that has plagued our country for the last several years began with the sudden rise and fall of stock prices and real estate values, and led to financial deflation, piles of massive nonperforming loans, an almost hopeless economy, a drop in tax revenues, worsening government finances, a rise in unemployment, credit uncertainty, the futile injection of public funds, a drag-down on the international economic system … and so on, *ad infinitum.* And if we compare real estate values in late twentieth century Japan to securities prices in pre-Depression America, although the causes and back-stories show subtle differences, we can rightly say that the pathogenesis and the ensuing pandemonium are fundamentally the same.

As Sonoyama's thesis was written in 1995, the real expansion and burst of the U.S. bubble had yet to occur. Now, not only has the U.S. repeated the mistakes it made 70 years ago and Japan had repeated in the early 1990s, but it is now recapitulating them on a global scale. Japan's particular brand of illusory capital was confined largely to domestic finances, which served to restrict the effects of Japan's bubble collapse mainly to Japan, thereby sparing the world a global meltdown. But the U.S. market is deeply interlinked with global finance, meaning that the fallout this time will be felt the world around, with the U.S. sitting square at the epicenter. We can expect that, within the next few years, the U.S. and world economy will devolve down lines very much like those that Japan slid down fifteen years ago.

The U.S. has tried to resist its own inexorable decline by launching a baseless war in Iraq, but we've all seen the poison fruit that bore. The hemorrhage just keeps spurting, and the economy seems doomed at this point. If the U.S. does go down, there's no way Europe will be able to provide the leadership needed to maintaining world order, and suddenly there will be no constabulary in the global village. Meanwhile, in an uncanny feat of bad timing the CCP has made capitalist economic success a national goal just as the wheels began to fly off, so the Chinese system will just be another domino to fall.

Looking back into Japanese history, we find that our current state of affairs is quite similar to that in Japan after the decline of the Muromachi *bakufu* government. As the power of the *bakufu* (and now, the U.S. government) waned, its ties with the regional lords appointed around Japan (allies of the U.S.) weakened. Soon the regional lords were unable to rule their territories, and eventually they ceded control to military warlords. This is our situation now, with the nations closest to the U.S. all trapped in its wake and swirling down.

When the 20th-century world order created by the U.S. and Europe fails, it will become imperative for the leaders of each country to be able to develop new means of livelihood for their citizens. That will be a struggle of politics, economy, international affairs, culture and thought that will require a full mobilization of nations to succeed. The leaders who rise up to this challenge will be the equivalents of the warlords of old, and from their ranks the next world leader may arise. The question is how to accomplish this in a peaceful, open manner; and the answers we arrive at will reveal just how much mankind has progressed in the last 600 years.

The collapse of an economic bubble, including Japan's and the current U.S. detumescence (perhaps triggered by the housing bubble air-loss in mid-2006 as these words are being written), carries the force to level economic and political systems on a global scale. However, the restoration of order in the wake of a bubble leads to rethinks and recalibrations, and the buildup that follows will be a wonderful opportunity for 21st century Japan and the world. What we need now is an economy based on a new philosophy, with a new currency and a new way of life—first for Japan and then, as soon as possible, for the rest of the world. I will talk more about the new system I envision in the chapters to follow, but it is important to note here that, until the new engine is up and running, until the system goes online, we will have to run both systems—the new, and the already-failing old one—simultaneously. There is a system for engineering railroad tracks such that the end of one section of rail gradually tapers just as the next section in line widens, so that the end of one runs immediately alongside the beginning of another for several yards, lessening the chances for catastrophic track breakage or derailment. This is how the transition from the ways of the 20th century to those of the 21st—from a death culture to lifestyles of health and sustainability—will play out. The old ways will gradually fade even as new ones come into existence and gather strength until they supplant the erstwhile order.

This gradual fade-in will be essential, for the majority of people in the world will of course undergo severe and in some cases irrecoverable shock when what they had perceived as wealth suddenly loses its value, which is what will happen when the US economy crashes, then hyperinflates (coming soon to a theatre near you). When that happens, if there are not yet any alternatives in place, the cumulative desperation would tear the world apart both financially and literally, and I am afraid we would be left with nothing. We need to have an alternative system in place to catch the pieces of the old as it disintegrates. Then, once the shift toward the new is progressing and the future economy is in sight, it will be time to offset all the old assets of the old system against our debts, and clean up the post-bubble mess once and for all. And as finance is a global system, this will need to be made happen simultaneously everywhere.

This must be accomplished by paying assets against accumulated debts. To make this transition happen, the rise, fall, life, and death of established organizations will, ironically, be left to market principles. No interventions; no propping up of zombie companies or subsidies for ancient bad loans; no Keynesian tweaking of prices and currency values. Laissez-faire means laissez-faire, and turnabout is fair play for the so-called proponents of free-marketism. By allowing market principles unfettered reign, we will allow the old system to die out naturally, while at the same time using pressure from the global market as a fulcrum or impetus to give individuals and organizations chances to undertake self-reform. It will be an evolutionary moment of extreme selective pressure. Those who are selected against must, through the hardships they will face before and after the transition, look deep within themselves and rethink their values, and ideals—all the fundamental human ideas that will become even more important in the new age—and learn how to put them into practice for themselves.

When thinking about organizational change, the first thing to keep in mind is that the world is always changing. All is flux; that's a truism that no one can deny. What we can do is either adapt to the changing times, or opt to resist. If a company thinks of nothing but the short-term bottom line, or if it clings to a particular business model, or attempts to maintain its former power, entitlements or image when that is no longer feasible, that behavior represents resistance to organizational change (resistance to change being the antonym of adaptation). If an organization resists change it will eventually cease to play a meaningful role in society or the economy. In other words, it will no longer be of any use, its very reasons for existence will disappear, and it will fail. For a corporation this means insolvency or breakup.

If the market mechanism is allowed to operate in this process, then not only will the process be rapid and relatively painless, but the market's unseen hand will assemble more useful organizations to replace the old, and any institutional adaptations that took place will succeed and evolve on a level that supersedes the life and death of any of the individual organizations involved. In a society that tolerates failures such as bankruptcies, an individual may, through the market mechanism, undergo multiple successes and failures and thereby develop a highly evolved management style. Regardless of whether these individuals initially possessed a clear, long-term vision, the end result is a society of people and organizations well adjusted through adaptation.

But when a bubble of the type described by Sonoyama occurs, the healthy market mechanism is compromised, and the popping of the bubble acts as a mass extinction event in the affected market. In this bleak scenario, management policies lacking in long-term vision temporarily appear to be shortcuts to success, and it becomes even harder to instill high-level management theory or a positive culture in a company or eliminate irresponsible behavior until eventually the entire company becomes morally bankrupt.

If, however, people within an organization embrace change, and they maintain discipline in their own self-reform, then that group stands a much better chance of surviving that particular round of natural selection and be able to grow and mature. Of course, not everyone will be able to reform and succeed. The new organization that has reformed must match the ideal selected for by the market mechanism. In other words, those organizations that change into something unlike what the market has selected for will fail, no matter how much energy they devote to self-reform. And remember, when I use the term market here, I'm not referring to the sucker's game of rigged markets we have now. I'm talking about a market in which viability is a factor of the benefit to the whole (society, mankind, the world), not simply shortsighted, hyper-competitive rivalries and plundering.

Self-reform in an organization is nothing less than a competition with the unseen hand of the market. Change is vital, but in a market where organizations are weeded out and reborn without artificial controls, the game is played for mortal stakes. However, if an organization wants to avoid natural selection in the market and adapt to the changing world through self-reform, it must evolve as fast or faster than the market itself. Self-reform also requires great foresight, the ability to see where the market is heading, while at the same time it requires leadership capable of enacting widespread and unlimited change at the organizational level. Only when this becomes prevalent will the relics of "free market" competition, natural (market) selection, and war disappear from the earth. If we want to avoid a conflict of the scale that Japan faced during the warring states period, we will need to have more foresight and better leadership than our predecessors of 600 years past.

It is unlikely, though, that our society will able to produce people capable of this kind of transformation by simply falling back on the sciences. Since the adversary, in this case, is the market *kami* (gods) themselves, any meaningful attempt at reform will have to address issues beyond the realm of science. Fallen as we are, we cannot hope to parley with deity. We will have to go back to theocracy, and the true meaning of a "unity of church and state" if we hope to produce a leader able to steer a course through these unfamiliar waters. Whether this happens now or later, more research on the potential of religion as a force in leadership and the (currently secular) market is necessary. These are uncomfortable words, I know, for a Japan that prides itself on its secularity, and its abandonment of past "superstitions" for its new faith in technology, rationality and scientific progress. But I ask my readers to look at where that unilateral rationalism has gotten us.

The new system I am speaking of is a system born from the experiences of those who have failed and those who have succeeded in the course of natural selection. While I will consider the policies and characteristics of that system in this text, the concrete details of the system itself must come out of the untidy chaos of people's encounters with change in the real world. Everyone will have to face the new system on his or her own terms, not as some dry and empty theory, but as a true process of self-reform. The important thing to remember is that they can succeed. We can all succeed.

Let me repeat that in order to cultivate this great sea change, we must not attempt to artificially influence the market mechanism. To do so is tempt the very real chance that everything (and I do mean everything) will die out in the aftermath of a massive economic meltdown. To avoid that global threat, each of us must undertake personal reform, a process that begins with the frank assessment of people as winners and losers (neither of which, remember, is a permanent state). As time passes, the gap between the two will grow; however, at the same time, countless interpersonal networks will naturally arise from the groups of people thrown together by the vagaries of their successes and failures. As the definition of success evolves, so will the taxonomies it supports.

In Japan in particular, this transformative process will likely cause the current vertically compartmentalized hierarchies to change into a vastly more horizon-

ends (at least for that round). But conversely, where there is a gathering of people with no strong self-interest and without deception, there is insufficient energy to generate a market system to begin with.

Sonoyama often compares the market to a nuclear reactor. If there are not enough people with the "radioactivity" of self-interest and deceit, there can be no reaction and thus no reactor. The current system works only by virtue of strict laws and the control system of regulatory agencies, intended to function as containment. Thanks to these controls, the danger of radiation leakage is controlled, and we can use it peacefully … most of the time. When the controls fail and the reaction goes wild, however, a bubble occurs, and when it breaks you have a meltdown. The solution? Take the radioactive uranium out of the reactor, and the reactor stops. If you can take self-interest and deception out of the market, the market will cease to function.

Sonoyama has pointed out that Japan's original system is like a waterwheel, where the members of a community use the gift of power from nature to support the entire community's livelihood. However, the "waterwheel" system alone leaves people unsatisfied. It is not enough that the daily blessings of nature are simply distributed among the community members. However, if we use a spiritual model instead of "manifest self-interest" to fuel the kind of leapfrogging change that people undertake in the market system when they pursue personal profit, then we will have the advantage of direct communication with the *kami*. If we add a continuous dialogue with the *kami* to the waterwheel system, then not only will it overcome the market system, but there will be no bubble. Our rewards will be intellectual, spiritual and cultural maturation, and a free pass out of the harsh cycle of natural selection. It will be a superior system, too, from the perspective of man's coexistence with nature.

The reason why Japan today cannot succeed within the global market mechanism is that, even though there are *kami*, or spiritual forces at work through the market mechanism (whether people realize it or not), the Japanese do not have the requisite attitude to fuel their own market mechanism and they do not consider the workings of the *kami*. As long as the status quo endures, the West will always have the market mechanism *kami* on their side, and we cannot hope to match them in either prediction or performance.

Under the new system, the market mechanism will cease to fulfill the central role it now plays. Particularly in Japan, even should the market mechanism fulfill its interim role of bringing down the current system, it will be of no use as a tool for making something new or evolutionary. A bubble collapse will only bring the current market system to a near standstill. It is self-evident that the new system will be brought to life by people who have succeeded in a reform that eschews the market mechanism altogether and derives its power instead from a spiritually informed leadership, the union of church and state.

Back to the Land

There is another concern, perhaps the most important, that the country will face as a new Japan is born. That is: what to do with those who fail, the dropouts that no one will want to work with. The solution we find will determine whether the coming global revolution will ultimately end in success or failure. To put it another way, it is not what the successful do that will make or break the new system, but what we do with the unsuccessful. If we end up with a system made by the victors that contains countless people who have failed and are dissatisfied with their lot, the system will become threatened, and there is a good chance that, as happened to our predecessors 600 years ago, our society will be plunged into war. As the dismantling of the old system progresses, it will become less able to support failure and the number of dropouts will increase. If at first we try to remedy the situation by lowering the threshold for success and mixing the failed in with the successful, in effect letting the victors' system prop up the less successful, the as-yet young new system will not be able to bear the strain, and everything will collapse again.

As the old system draws nearer to its natural death, a time in which we have to nurture the unsteady new system, we will need a place to hold the unsuccessful, to absorb the large number of failures that will result from the reforms. This catchment cannot be part of the old system nor the new. After the end of the war in 1945, people who lost their factory jobs with the collapse of the war industry went back to the countryside to work on farms, and then once sustained economic growth had gotten the cities back on track, they filtered back into the factories to join the ranks of the new economy. Thus we see that, during the 20 years between the end of the wartime economy and the new peaceful export industry began, agriculture served as a temporary holding place for workers from the failed factories.

I suggest we learn from this history and make agriculture our safety net once again. The land can be a temporary reservoir for absorbing the failures of the old system. For those who are left without employment in the reform, this will be a chance to take their own sustenance from the earth itself, the chance to be part of a family farm. Modern society in Japan and the rest of the world has come to an impasse in its agricultural policies. The friction surrounding agricultural trade is unending; there is a tremendous amount of overproduction and failed crops, and we see danger to our food industry in modern plagues like mad cow disease and avian flu. To me, this indicates that agriculture is incompatible with a money-centric economy. We do not trust the currency to raise our own children, shouldn't we have a similar distrust of it to provide what we eat? People freely spend time and money on raising and educating their children, is it not just as natural for us to spend time, effort and money growing the food we eat?

For those who have failed, it is of paramount importance to help them form stable networks with others, or to participate in extant networks. Ultimately, they will find work through these networks, naturally gaining the ability to part fully in the new system. However, achieving employment through the improvement of an individual's marketable skills is not the only goal of this kind of rehabilitation. As I mentioned previously, networks are distinguished by their member's spiritu-ality, their thoughts, or to put it another way, their closeness to the governing *kami*. Thus we see that our first priority is to instill those who have failed with a renewed higher level of spirituality.

Ideally, our reservoir for the unsuccessful must on the one hand ensure that people's most basic needs will be met without requiring support from the old market system, and on the other, it must nurture their spirituality during the time they spend there. This point in particular distinguishes this solution from current efforts to assist the unemployed, which tend only to reinforce helplessness and dependency.

In the end, everything comes back to the land.

The land quietly decomposes all that is rotten or unneeded, rendering it harm-less, and then turning it into nutrients to feed new life. All plants on this earth come from the land, and the earth has sufficient nutrients to sustain every plant. If we think of unsuccessful approaches (be they individual lives or organizational structures) as futureless and inutile, and if we think of a network as a place for new life, then the interval between a person's failure in the old system and their rebirth in the new resembles the natural decomposition and transformation into new nourishment by the land. If you fail in the old system, you let your current form go to compost, then, given the right environmental conditions, you will gradually find yourself refashioned into a productive and fulfilled participant in the new society. It's the organic alchemy of the earth. All you have to do is wait for the conditions to manifest.

When people make what they eat from the land, they pour their hearts into growing their food, for they want to eat good things. Then, when what they have grown is tasty enough, they eat it, robbing that plant of life. When you make what you will eat from the ground, it makes you think in a very direct and visceral way about the meaning of life and death. You give love to something only to kill it, and therein lies an important key to understanding mortality. Working the land is a path to spirituality that the new system has effectively put out of most people's reach.

The rehabilitating function of the land is vital to the infrastructure of the coming age. Enabling everyone to farm for their personal consumption not only enriches a society, but new interpersonal associations will be born and disappear as if of their own volition, and in these rising and falling horizontal societies, there is a need for a place to care for people in the time between the death of one era and its rebirth in a new form. That is the role of the land.

The working world, then, becomes a great farm built upon this foundation of the land. On this farm, each corporation or group is like a plant with its own unique role and vision. They co-exist and thrive by gathering people's energy together towards one objective. The home, schools, and regional networks must serve as the nurseries. Above and beyond what they may consider their relevant duties now, they must give first priority to healing and accept the ranks of the beaten and failed. They can, in part, fulfill the role of the land by healing and re-educating people, or simply by letting them rest peacefully while cultivating and preserving their knowledge. The exurban regions can provide homes for people to gather their powers and wait for their next foray into the world beyond. Plants, too, participate in a waste-free cycle only when they enjoy the fruits of the earth's great power to decompose and recycle, and in this we can see a truth of life that applies equally to us.

In the 20th century, we too often paid homage to ruthless efficiency in organizations, i.e. the plants, and paid little respect to other functions of the earth. As a result, the natural cycle is breaking down, air is choked with pollution, the water dirty and becoming scarce, and societies burdened with unemployment and economic instability. In many senses, all our vaunted progress has only made our lives worse.

The new age for Japan and the world must now first play the part of the earth, mulching the dead plants into fertile soil so that a new world of life can spring forth. In societal terms, this can best be achieved by a return to agriculture, giving people a chance to grow food for themselves. Agriculture, not plunder, must become the foundation of the new society.

The Ministry of Agriculture, Forestry and Fisheries recently published a study showing what kind of diet we can look forward to if Japan's food imports were to be cut off. Dinner would be a bowl of rice, a baked sweet potato and some fish. We could enjoy *miso* soup every other day, and meat once every nine days. Unexciting fare, but although it may be lacking in variety, the menu includes nutritious items from all the major food groups and indicates that the Japanese would be able to continue living balanced and healthy lives even if they had to abandon their current, nearly gluttonous, ways. With the world scene being what it is, the chances of Japan losing its access to foreign crude oil or foodstuffs are not as remote as we might like to think.

Given those risks, this is no time to get caught up in hurried misadventures; we need to make real changes in our approach to the use of energy and food. Now is the time to start planning for how to deal with a potential stoppage of trade, and not just by looking at the troubles that are sitting right in front of us; we need a hundred year plan that will let us start preparing for a fresh new start in the way we operate. The tree pollen situation is worse this year that it's ever been, and we're seeing lots of new allergy sufferers. The only solution seems to be to cut the trees down. Beginning every spring day with a dose of pills and the donning of goggles and a mask is not a viable option. If we lose our access to oil, we could harvest the trees and use them to develop an alternative fuel source, making sure to reforest mountainous areas that have been logged. If we're going to build a strong new future from the ashes of our outworn attitudes and habits, it's time for us to step up the pace and get to work.

A Return to Quality

While educating the populace on understanding the vital roles played by the earth, Japan must begin, at every level, to bring together the people and knowledge to effect the systemic and regulatory reforms that will be needed to reassign public and some privately owned land to farmland, and the necessary agricultural technology and methods to produce enough food to support life. Only when the nation revives the life-giving role of the land will it have an eternal life, and at that time we can say that the rebuilding of Japan is complete. The next step then will be to share that knowledge and capability with the world.

Looking at the directions in which China and India are now developing, the inevitable conclusion is that Japan cannot hope to continue in industries in which the mass production and wholesale distribution of goods is the goal. As for China and India, if they do not succeed in making sustainable societies of their own, then their own lives and livelihoods will be threatened, and the global age of industrial manufacturing may come to a close.

If we think of the making of tools and technologies as the foundation of industry, we realize that there is a need to make easier-to-use, longer-lasting tools. Think about Japanese swords or tea bowls. The sense of value and quality we feel from these objects comes from the high degree of spiritual contribution to their creation. Now, look at the consumer habits of the Japanese today, and you might be surprised by the amount of goods and services offered for the sole purpose of creating peace of mind. From "healing" services like aromatherapy and massage, to complementary medical clinics and slow food restaurants, to organic food suppliers and interior products designed to create a soothing ambience. As one might expect from the most advanced nation in the world, Japanese consumers look first to their consumer lifestyle for spiritual fulfillment. They seek to buy their way into lifestyles of health and sustainability, as if guided by some instinct.

An excellent guide for us to follow when building our new society then is Japan's tradition of fusing material culture with spiritual culture—a tradition that we see, with the modern Japanese looking for peace of mind in consumerism, is very much alive. Thus it will be possible to build the coming Japan on the basis of Japanese traditional culture. Looking at the world today we see how vital this is. The current age is one of food and tools devoid of spirituality. Things lack soul. Even should we consume them, we are not truly satisfied on a spiritual level, and as we see from the number of problems in the world resulting from dissatisfaction or uneasiness, we realize that it will not possible for us to create a new world if we ignore the needs of the spirit.

We must use tools to satisfy both our material needs and cultivate our spiritual natures. To fill this need, Japan's world-leading manufacturing industry need to return to making things with high artistic value. Japan must rediscover its roots in quality and attention to detail. At the same time, the manufacturing workforce will necessarily decrease to occupy a far smaller percentage of the population than it does today, with bespoke products and the manufacture of fewer models in smaller lots becoming the norm. Quality, not quantity, will be key. To enable this, programs will have to be established to guide future craftsmen through a lengthy course of study and apprenticeship during which they learn to make objects with a real investment of spirit. The days of the impersonal production line are waning.

As farming for domestic consumption and the creation of spiritually meaningful goods and technologies spreads, we will have made for ourselves a society that truly plays the part of the land. General education, too, must be refined to emphasize those elements that will actively help build this society. Curricula will be remade from the bottom up, with the questions of when, where and how to teach each individual to maximize their potential for success asked at every stage. Then, once we establish a base of leadership for running a horizontal society, Japan will have the strength and flexibility to respond and adapt to changes in the world, and will have true regenerative potential and thus, eternal life, of a sort. That is true sustainabaility; health everlasting.

If we do this, Japanese will truly lead graceful lives, and people will come from around the world to experience the wonders of new society firsthand and interact with the Japanese for themselves. The basis for sustainable tourism is not to emphasize going to a place to see unusual sights (the wonder of which quickly runs out, sometimes the victim of its own success), but instead to meet the people who live there. If Japan is to live up to its reputation as one of the most advanced nations on earth and be the first to introduce a new way of life that transcends the outmoded values of the 20th century, then our society will be a like a bright and unwavering light, and people will come to literally see that light, and bask in its warmth and glow.

Its emphasis on receiving guests with hospitality and warmth is one of Japan's great cultural achievements and source of pride and strength; when foreign visi-

long run, it is not always the right choice to follow the tenet of "the customer is king" and give him what he asks for without considering what it is he really needs.

In the coming economy, it will be imperative for merchants to engage with their customers as equals. It will also be the merchant's responsibility to choose customers who will trust him enough to make such a relationship possible. If, for instance, as a clothes salesman you are entrusted with clothing a customer and his family, you must consider each family member's taste, age, social standing, lifestyles and budget, all with the same care that you would show when clothing your own family. In return, the customer will reward this total care and service by not putting your business at risk by demanding lower prices or by going to another merchant. Why should they, when you are the best-qualified person to provide them their ideal service? The customer benefits by avoiding other merchants who might ply them with inferior products, for they know that it is better to spend a little more on something of quality than waste money on a cheap product that will soon deteriorate or break. This arrangement also saves them time worrying about what to buy.

This kind of client relationship can be summed up in the word *goyotashi*. No matter what the product or service, the concept of an exclusive purveyor for each need is a powerful concept that will prove central in the coming years. A *goyotashi* merchant needs to know everything about his or her customers. Their relationship with the customer goes beyond providing goods and services; it is first and foremost a human relationship, and only secondarily an avenue for sales. The *goyotashi* merchant takes the time to visit customers' homes, and connects with them on a number of different levels. In the course of this daily contact, the merchant is constantly considering the best products and services for their customers. When such a relationship is established, the continuing care for a product after it has been sold will become a matter of course. And the more skilled the merchant at developing a sense of his customers' true wants and needs, the broader the range their *goyotashi* services can have. A purveyor of clothes might expand to provide sporting goods or accessories. The more the seller knows about the buyer's home, taste in food and cars, and idiosyncrasies, the more of these things they can provide in an effective manner until they are providing every service the customer requires. The more the merchant responds faithfully to a customer's individual needs, the stronger the relationship between the two becomes, until the risk of competition is minimized. This is what is meant by commitments: each is committed to the other. Committed service on the part of the *goyotashi*, and a commitment of loyalty on the part of the customer.

Prices, too, become secondary in this system. The cost of time spent to understand the customer's needs, the cost of maintaining channels of communication between you and the customer, and indeed the possible rewards to the purveyor are not measurable in terms of money. In a society where everyone supports each other, society itself becomes a kind of welfare insurance. The cost of one particular item loses much of its meaning. Which is to say, that, price aside, no one is able to say exactly what the true cost of any product is. The concept of value itself must be redefined. In the new economy, value will derive from quality, commitment and service, not price tags.

This kind of *goyotashi* system would be very difficult to establish and maintain in a period of dramatic economic growth. When the economy is booming, and opportunities to get rich abound, no one has the time to spend getting to know any one customer. Customers become nothing more than a set of objects to be processed. In such an environment, people try to shed responsibilities so that they have the freedom to cultivate their own talents for personal enrichment and achieve the greatest possible individual success. A premium is placed on selfishness.

But when the economy slows, monetary wealth and career advancement lose their luster. When even a simple, ordinary life becomes hard to sustain, a world in which people treat each other as soulless objects becomes very unstable indeed. In such times, it is necessary to make the switch to the *goyotashi* culture of interlinked commitments, and nurture instead the ability to acknowledge and respect the richness of each and every customer's individuality. Being a merchant is suddenly less about selling a product, it is about developing a relationship with another human being, and, as a professional, helping them live the best possible life and eventually becoming trusted to provide for all of their needs.

When an economic slump continues for so long that the next generation cannot hope to live as richly as their parents, in the interests of their own security children would be much more willing to listen to what their parents had to say, and where possible, they would seek to follow in their parents' footsteps in their own careers. It would be difficult for them to consider doing otherwise. If they take over the family business, they would likely have the same customers as did their parents. Those customers would in turn be likely to continue to give them their patronage. If the relationship between merchant and customer is a familiar one, the children would already know the customer's needs, and the customer would be relieved to not have to search out a new merchant. Far from being unstable, this kind of relationship ensures that business will continue as usual, even in hard times. It would not be odd for a *goyotashi* relationship like this to continue over the course of many generations. Any buildup of capital then becomes a escape hatch, if needed, for those who wish to break out of the *goyotashi* relationship and explore new opportunities elsewhere. But that will only be possible for many after the new age has fully been ushered in. The cycle continues to turn and the pendulum swings endlessly.

In the current economy, discount stores selling to anonymous customers are flourishing, but as the economy moves towards a *goyotashi* regime, these establishments are bound to gradually disappear. We will soon bid farewell to the 100-yen shop. You cannot continuously discount items without someone somewhere taking a loss, and, Say's Law notwithstanding, production does not necessarily create its own demand. Furthermore, since in the big box, cost-cutting mindset, where customers can sense they are mere faceless units to the corporations that sell to them, they lack any sense of long-term loyalty. As soon as it becomes difficult for the seller to drop its prices, the relationship is over. Nothing is harsher than price competition in an age of slow economic growth.

Once the economy has been transformed into the *goyotashi* mode, treatment of customers as the great unwashed will cease. The financial world now too, objectifies its clients, but this is the thinking of the aristocracy for peasants; it has no place in an enlightened and egalitarian world. There is *goyotashi* finance, just as there is *goyotashi* trade. High-risk commodities such as stocks should only be sold to buyers who are fully apprised of and able to assume the risk. They should certainly not be sold blindly to the faceless masses. It is precisely this kind of chancemedley selling on the part of brokerages that has led the economy to falter. Brokers need to learn how to refuse customers. How's that for a revolution in thinking? Treating one's customers as unknown masses should be strictly forbidden; there needs to be a basic rethinking of the traits and standards by which customers are evaluated and a full review of the risk and return potentials of currently existing commodities.

Realizing the Goyotashi Economy

So, with the achievement of a *goyotashi* system as our economic goal, how should we proceed? Currently, the few places that can truly be called *goyotashi* purveyors maintain their privileged position by virtue of their considerable monetary resources and the weight of tradition. In order to make *goyotashi* feasible for everyone, we need to make quality products cheaply. This requires artful management. One cannot succeed by clinging to the reasoning that cheap means third rate. The whole idea of having to settle for inferior quality while others enjoy the best is insulting to the customer. The principle at work there is face-smackingly obvious: those who are not rich should have lower quality service, and the less money you have, the lower the grade of service you deserve. However, the fact that the customer is forced to look in his wallet and select a lower grade for himself is even more degrading and offensive. Nobody wants to go into a restaurant offering a range of deluxe menu items and then be forced to choose peasant fare.

Of course, there is no point to taking a loss just for the sake of cutting prices; that's an unsustainable approach to doing business. In order to lower a price, you need to cut features. Instead of dropping the overall quality of a product, identify the product's main features, and then trim away all that is irrelevant. The tendency in Japan tends to be to try to make everything the ultimate product in every conceivable category or function, but that invariably results in only ordinary products being made.

For example, when designing a car intended for a new college grad, it is sufficient to have a safe vehicle that they can ride in with their friends. You can dispose of all other features and still have a product that meets that customer's needs. And by trimming away unnecessary options, the maker can afford to meet the same safety standards used for a luxury vehicle. The age group most likely to die in vehicular accidents is young drivers in their teens and twenties. They like to drive fast. More than any other group, they need access to safe cars. The merchant that sells them that first car can become their *goyotashi*, a trusted source, known for considering individual needs and providing vehicles that keep pace with changes in their income, their lifestyles and newly available technologies.

I believe we must put the utmost effort into rethinking the automobile and the framework that surrounds it. The most expensive thing most people will ever buy is a house, and the second most expensive is a car. Once bought, a house can be used for a lifetime, and if you own the land beneath it, it is conceivable that your children might live there as well, and theirs after them. But even though cars are the second most expensive items that the average person buys, they are treated much like disposable goods. For the average Japanese car, its market value drops to zero only six years after purchase. You could certainly keep driving it longer than six years, but it would no longer have value as a resalable item. It's not that the car is undriveable—many of the best cars can run for fifteen or twenty years. It's just that the framework encourages people to continually buy new cars every few year. It's a function of the laws, the economic structure of the country and the prevailing mindset with its emphasis on consumerism.

This is unacceptable. Expensive products should have a long useable lifespan. Cars should be made with to hold their value for ten, even twenty years. They should be made modifiable to adapt to changes in income and lifestyle, and people should be encourage to hold onto their cars, maintain them and continue to enjoy them for many years. The kind of individual care needed to modify an automobile is impossible in a price-driven economy that values volume sales, but in a *goyotashi* economy, it becomes necessary to hand-craft the perfect car for each individual customer. This also gives the retailer and the maker the freedom and latitude to express individuality and add value to the product. If you forgo market expansion, there is no limit to the extent of personalized service you can provide.

If the maker of automobiles wishes to succeed in the future, then the first car they design needs to be something that is the realization of the hopes and dreams of that recent grad. Imagine the impact it would have if a carmaker could manufacture the kind of automobile that everyone dreams of having, but has given up on because of the cost. Of course, there is something to be said for starting small, but we want a merchant with a little guts, someone who will give us our dreams. A dream car is, and can only be, a work of art. The *goyotashi* maker needs to decide what features it will have and strip away absolutely everything else. At the same time, he or she must also leave room open for future modifications. This gives secondary and tertiary providers opportunities for future business, making improvements on the original product. The automobile industry is the cornerstone of a whole group of related industries; successfully introducing this kind of concept in car design and manufacture would have an effect on the entire national economy, which even now centers on the automobile. The dream car would be more than a product, it would signal a change in the times, and give us all hopes and dreams for a new future. It is evolutions such as these, which seem local and perhaps mundane in their immediate effects, that will work together to bring about the *goyotashi* restoration.

Values and Visions for Tomorrow

Our think tank recently held what we called the Hinata-mura Festival, the first event of its kind, welcoming visitors male and female, young and old. The name Hinata-mura comes from the name of a virtual village referred to in summer and snow festivals as part of a leadership game we also conduct, and in the Hinata-mura festival our staff played the parts of Hinata villagers, providing some of the knowledge and materiel needed for life in the new age we live in.

The day was a full one, with gardening, a seafood and vegetable barbecue, *mochi* rice-cakes, *udon* and *miso*, sampling of a variety of regional soy sauces, and sundry arts and crafts. For me, and I suspect others as well, the event was a direct experience both of the ideals of the coming age, in which individuals live and collaborate with each other and with the natural world, each finding and thriving in his or her own path, as well as of the power to melt away any resistance in the hearts and minds of the doubtful and the stubborn.

The day also served as a real demonstration that the information that will lead to Lifestyles of Health and Sustainability can't be had entirely from digital media; analog sources are equally important and necessary. Think about it for a moment and I believe you'll appreciate how true that is. Can't you feel the difference between store-bought bread and that which you've kneaded and baked yourself? Or taste the difference between food cooked on a gas range and food that has been grilled over charcoal? You can only really understand the difference by experiencing it for yourself, and that is the 21st century version of luxury. In this century ahead, the accrual of analog experiences—knowing, going, seeing and meeting firsthand—will be paramount. In fact, the only way to understand the life of the new century is to live it; it's not something that can be grasped in a purely intellectual way. That's important to remember. You can't understand the 21st century using your head alone.

An NPO in which I serve as a director is now pushing ahead with an initiative based on that "Know-Go-See-Meet" paradigm to promote a new LOHAS-friendly country, a Great Collaboration in Japan by identifying and implementing effective investment and education. One part of that involves the development of a new financial system, an effort that involves analog knowledge sharing by people who already know the realities of extant financial systems inside and out. I've begun to see a recent flourishing, where the energy imparted by a LOHAS way of life has translated into wellbeing and happiness for individuals, and at the same I am saddened when I see those suffering and depressed because they aren't able to tap into those feelings. What Japan needs now is a new investment bank, with the funds needed to back small startups, even a system of micro-loans, and the independence and ability to give the country a much-needed boost to its fiscal air defense. Money will not be everything, but it will still be important, and the country needs to develop its financial infrastructure to protect itself from the carpet-bombing and siege warfare tactics of global capital, and to provide for the needs of its individual citizens and businesspeople.

People may tell you that Japan enjoys a healthy economy these days, but if you factor out a few exceptionally strong firms, the picture is more of a boom among secondary industries lifted by the swollen tide of the Chinese manufacturing bubble. Primary and tertiary industries remain in their protracted slump. Even worse, the emptying out of the countryside for the urbs goes on and a look at the real estate price index shows that even as average prices for land in commercial districts in the biggest three metropolitan areas in the country have recently gone up for the first time in 15 years, there are many more regions when they continue to fall. The key question in building a new Japanese economy will be how to stimulate primary and tertiary industry in the regional prefectures, with the requisite leadership, guidance and injections of capital.

The primary industries are agriculture, fishing, forestry and other forms of resource extraction, and it seems natural that their successful regional revival would hinge upon sophisticated agriculture capable of yielding value-added, high-end produce. Encouraging resettlement the exurbs among the coming generation of retirees could help to boost populations, and the development of multi-purpose farming, and the full and judicious use of land, sea, rivers and lakes will also be fundamental. In the non-urban regions, I would say that tourism represents the only viable driver of tertiary industrial growth.

The crucial thing will be for both primary and tertiary industry to realize what our secondary industry manufacturers have already achieved—producing quality recognized the world around. For lifestyles and sightseeing attractions, just as for products, the regions need to maintain a constant awareness of the world's highest standards when developing their own offerings. If that is done, Japan's regional economies will surely revive and thrive as a result. Collusive price-fixing, quality compromises or other interregional connivance would be a fatal mistake, a mutual suicide pact for economies that need to surpass (not merely achieve) the highest quality standards if they are to survive.

There is no reason that Japan, with its fertile soil and culture and traditions born of a long, rich history, cannot become a world leader in both agriculture and tourism if it but uses the gifts with which it has been blessed. The only thing left for the country is to work out a post-Koizumi course for itself, and with the rejection of the current administration's ways and means already revving into overdrive, now we need to turn to developing a dynamic and fruitful interaction once again between the government and the economy.

At the same time, I think it will be vital for everyone—individuals of working age, students, children and retirees alike—to take at least one day a week, Saturday for example, and spend it in studying and learning for themselves about how to live and thrive in the 21st century mode. No matter how busy, they need to set aside time once a week on a Saturday to learn these basics of living in the new age. Students, children and pensioners also need to take to the time in the same ways to explore ways of breaking out of their respective molds. People locked in their workaholism, their getting and spending and the vicious speed-crazy cycle of rushing to meet deadlines that only force you to hurry more, need to begin by learning just how to make time for themselves. Make your time, use it for learning and meeting new people; these are the first steps toward becoming a thriving citizen of the 21st century. If we all agree on time to study and learn together, that will be the beginning of a network of collaboration and symbiosis for the new century.

The Japanese language has long used the words *hare* and *ke* to distinguish between special events and everyday routine, such as work or school. *Hare* and *ke* represent complementary opposites, whose balanced alternation gives rise to a healthy rhythm for human activity. A life of uninterrupted *ke* would be deadening, while one of all *hare* would equally stand to wear anyone out. In Japan, the IT revolution that promised to lighten workloads both in the office and at home seems only to have resulted in the transformation of the passage of time into an undifferentiated succession of days. A look at any schedule book makes clear the priority given to work, with the hare of family and community events relegated to the back burner. The net effect is only a widespread sense of depression. In the past, Japan wisely maintained a calendar of annual festivals and year-end holidays that maintained a healthy balance between *hare* and *ke* against the backdrop of the changing seasons. Hasn't the time come for these same people to put aside their worries over whether this year's sales or income will be higher than last and abandon the almost comically single-minded myth of progress, and instead enjoy that time they have and achieve the serenity to allow them to strive after their life's true goals with a charged sense of purpose.

In order to restore that balance, people need to learn to manage their time more wisely, and by that I mean giving themselves time for life, for learning and relaxation, for simple enjoyment. As part of our own corporate education, the staff of our company has leased some farmland in Odawara and we've started keeping a vegetable garden there. The person in charge of maintaining it rides a motorbike up the mountain to get there. In the Showa Era, production, making things, was the leading edge of the Japanese economy, and in the 1990s, the Internet transformed the country.

In the 21st century, it will be tourism and agriculture that change Japan yet again. If we're not careful, the youngest generation will just get pigeonholed into existing systems and forced to toil away under relentless management, but we should see that theirs is just the energy that's needed to build new and creative production solutions. Japan's population has dropped in two consecutive months since the start of this year and the consequences of living in a society undergoing net demographic shrinkage are now all but inevitable. This is a time for quality over quantity. We need to rethink the Japanese approaches to production, education and domestic development that till now have emphasized maximum volume, and devise new strategies that instead will put improving quality first. If we stick with the idea that, if we can't move enough units here, we have to export them overseas, we'll never extract ourselves from the fierce competition in the global markets and we could all one day end up like the big electronics makers—drowning in red ink and utterly spent.

The recent undervaluing of the yen has meant that Japan sees 20 trillion yen flush out into the international stock markets every year, while the Bank of Japan prints money like there's no tomorrow to back its bonds. While wealth pours out of the country in the scam of weak yen rates, cheap money makes the rounds by the bale at home. Is it just me, or does this strike anybody else as a spitting image of the last days of the Edo Period? Once the critical point is reached, we're going to see just what they saw at the end of the *bakufu*: hyperinflation, a change in government, and revolutions in law and praxis.

Japan actually holds great capital right now. Despite all the funds we've hemorrhaged overseas, we still possess wealth. Call it a weak economy if you want, but we still enjoy the fruits of land and sea from around the world, and people still live their lives more or less in comfort. That's why it's important for us to do something before the Koizumi reforms tear up our wealth roots and all and port it off to foreign lands; we need to build a better system from within, find ways of using the money that's disappearing overseas more wisely at home and make a new country from the old. We already have the people, the funds, the technologies needed to build a new Japan for the new century right here at home. This is the biggest difference between Japan today and at the end of the shogunate. All we lack is new leadership. Deficits alone cannot precipitate a true crisis; only when they exceed the ability of the leaders of the day do they become actively dangerous. Leaders, not numbers. And when I speak of a true leader, I mean someone who combines the ability to arrest decline, through strength of personality, vision and ability. It's only when a country's troubles exceed the capacity of its leaders that hope for the nation is lost.

How has Japan been served for leaders in the 21st century so far? I'd say we've seen more than our share of Leadership Lite. There's been no sign of the kinds of leaders that inspire the sense of reassurance that, come what may, they'll handle it. The past few years of leadership has been more and more like watching a bunch of kids playing at the beach with their shovels and pails, immensely pleased with themselves for building sand castles at low tide, completely unaware of what will happen when the waves start to roll in. There doesn't seem to be any simple solution at this point.

Or is there? I believe the solution is new leadership.

At the end of the Edo Period, the famous Sontoku Ninomiya developed a system of pragmatic approaches that came to be known as *shihou* for the reform of the feudal clan system. The following quote is from a book by Keiji Kamitani, *Jo no michi—Ninomiya Sontoku no iinokoshita koto* (The Way of Concession: Lessons from Sontoku Ninomiya) published in 1992 by ABC Publications; it's long, but it has such relevance to the current situation in Japan that I'm citing it here in full.

> When Ninomiya began to put the shihou into practice, he first sought to win over the *daimyo* leaders of the feudal households and change their way of thinking. If he just told servants from a given household that their lord had said he wanted to implement the *shihou* method in his fief, it was not easy to get them to comply. So he tried to persuade the lords that the implementation was their own (the *daimyo*'s) responsibility. He understood that if he wanted the reforms to work, he needed to be able to speak directly with the elders of the households and convince them of the value of the *shihou* system. Ninomiya understood that shihou was not merely an economic reform, but a change in the way people thought and felt. He waited until he was sure that the *daimyo* had truly understood and appreciated the nature of the system before moving forward with the implementation. His plan was rooted in an understanding of the relationship between the *daimyo*, his servants and the

peasantry. This was a time when servants were not regarded as having independent thoughts or minds, and farmers were viewed as little more than slaves. Ninomiya laid out the whole plan to the *daimyo*, from the rule of heaven to the ways of man, leading along them to the conclusion that their fiefdoms could not be maintained without the servants and farmers. He made them concede that, though their standing in society may differ, each person, be he servant or peasant, has a value and role to play as an individual. Once he succeeded in winning the *daimyo* over to that way of thinking, he moved to put *shihou* into practice.

Later, when he assessed the annual taxes on individual plots, he was able to plot out an economic map of the land under the *shihou* system, which allowed him to prove to the *daimyo* that the tax burdens to date had been unreasonably high, convincing them to lower taxes as a result. The key was in first getting the *daimyo* to concede. At the same time, Ninomiya succeeded in inspiring the peasantry and convincing them to change their ways of thinking. He met with the farmers, acknowledging their importance and the fact that, without them the feudal system (society) itself could not be maintained, and set about reviewing the tax system, developing a more reasonable tax collection system, and instilling a sense that the feudal system was not simply a collection racket by establishing local government offices where peasants could make their opinions heard. This had the effect of demonstrating that their lords also recognized their important role in the society and their value as individuals. The farmers themselves became more motivated by the sense of purpose gained from seeing the importance of their own contribution to society, and they gradually accepted and integrated the new system into their work and lives. As the need for taxation was clear, each individual came to understand his lot.

What do you think of that? Try substituting "ministers" or "CEOs" for the *daimyo*, and "citizens" or "employees" for the peasantry and the example can be applied exactly to our world today. If a leader such as this emerges, then we may see the birth of a new Japan.

A strong leader can prevail. The betrayers of the nation don't have the spirit they used to. Or rather, the people running the government these days have already exhausted any possible excuse when the big lies finally get exposed. And that means they intend to keep on lying right up to the end, and then jump sides once the truth becomes known. When you have the Finance Minister saying that the bad loans situation has been resolved, you can get away from it when the real truth comes out. But they also know that the revelation of the truth will mean the collapse of Japanese assets and finances, which will put Japan under the governance of the American and Chinese-operated IMF. So it seems here we have this group of people eagerly looking forward to becoming IMF axe-men and flunkies.

They may be taking a beating right now at the hands of the public, the press and the world, but aren't they looking forward to the day when, after tearing their own country down, they can climb into the enemy bed and snuggle up to the IMF and hold on to their own authority by getting appointed as custodians?

Sixty years ago, following the end of World War II, the Treasury Minister issued temporary payments to cover the costs of Allied forces two weeks after the end of hostilities on August 15, and three weeks later an account was opened for the Allies in the Bank of Japan at the order of the GHQ, and then on October 1st, the BOJ was effectively rendered unable to stay open for business after the site was appropriated and its precious metals put under Occupation control. Japan today has already passed its own August 15 surrender and now faces a new October 1st BOJ seizure by stealth, but this time there are people trying to keep themselves in power by showing their fealty in exchange for the promise of appointment as caretakers of the new Occupation and doggishly seeking attaboys and pats on the head.

When the Tokugawa *bakufu* went belly up, the bureaucrats lost no time in tossing out Chinese edicts and Confucianism, and people quickly turned to Western learning. After the Second World War as well, people dropped the fabrications of Japanese mythology and began to study the social sciences. And now, once people begin to realize that the teachings of pinnacles of the university education system as seen on Tokyo and Keio have been leading the country to its destruction, they'll toss out modern economics, financial theories, political science, law and the whole architecture that Tokyo U. sits perched atop and begin the search for new ways of understanding the world.

What a mess. But getting the foreign crooks out of Japan is actually an easy thing to do. An honest look at Japan's situation today reveals a scenario in which the real crooks are in cahoots with minor apparatchiks and worker drones in a scheme targeting the wealthy, who have taken out loans using their personal assets as collateral, allowing the swindlers to pressure and squeeze their stooges into handing over the collateral in lieu of repayment. It's really a simple problem to solve. Kick out the stooges and get rid of the debt. Specifically, issue lots of new money, which will have the effect of dropping both debts and savings back down to zero, erasing obligations without incurring any stigma.

This can work because Japan's ultra-rich have many assets other than purely fiscal ones, such as technology, know-how and rich land, that bear no relation to finance. Reduce the yen to wastepaper and that wealth will still remain, and region-by-region Japan will begin to develop new currencies and a new national outlook. The predators are interested in more than just the 1.4 quadrillion yen in

Japanese monetary wealth; their ultimate aim is to acquire the true Japanese assets that lie hidden behind. That's why the crooks try to keep Japan from issuing new money through the threat of freezing assets or raising taxes. If prices were to rise tenfold, 350 trillion in postal savings would suddenly be worth only 35 trillion; a hundredfold would leave them at only 3.5. The biggest problem with the hyper-inflation solution is that, while the money still has some value, foreign opportunists will be looking to cart off or lay claim to Japan's assets lock, stock and barrel.

So how can we get the administrators under the swindler's thumb to start printing money? That's easy to. All we need is for the Japanese people under a few new leaders to come out and start talking honestly about what they already know. General public disclosure. Of course the crooks will attempt a clampdown using confidentiality agreements and threats of defamation actions, but if we succeed in getting rid of them, the people made criminals for speaking the truth will become heroes overnight. And once the truth is out, the administrators and functionaries won't be able to do anything but print and issue money by the reams in an attempt at public appeasement. And by playing the card of strategic hyperinflation, Japan will have rid itself of the legion of foreign crooks (which indeed was the stratagem used by Europe to drive out the American felons during the Russian crisis in 1998). And at the same time, it will signal a changing of the guard for both the big and little fish who have been running the domestic show, fueling a New Deal for a new Japan. (Unfortunately, in Russia's case, their New Deal led straight down the path to militarism.)

In the absence of such capable leaders, people aren't showing much interest in the concept of creating Japan completely anew. And that's the biggest problem of all. They also need to recognize that the principles that apply to things newly born are totally different from those that apply to things ongoing. We need more soft-power evangelism; we need more buy-in. For instance, the economy runs on the principle of the exchange of equivalent value, but when an economy first springs forth, it is only through the contributions of nature, of parents and power holders with their money and technology, that make the preparation for that exchange of equity possible. In essence, to launch an economy *ab initio* requires donations, economic asymmetries; in the joint stock system, the shareholders are the donors. Even in our own economy, the financial value of nature's contributions has been calculated at tens of trillions of dollars, which goes completely unrecognized and unaccounted for. The problem for publicly owned companies is, now it isn't clear whether stock owners are acting as actual contributors or are just in it for self-serving money grabs that chew up businesses whole, leaving them unable to carry on fulfill what should be their true missions of service and quality creation. It is a sure road to failure for both the companies themselves and the economy as a whole.

If we compare cell and traditional phones, do we see the cell phone as a traditional phone that gradually lost its tail (phone cable) in some kind of evolutionary process? Obviously not. The cell phone arose when someone had the idea of combining the merits of wireless and conventional telephones. Cell phones could come into being only because someone dreamt the concept up. Then, to realize that concept, they borrowed some of the features of both wireless and standard wire-bearing phones and combined them in a new device. Again, for anything new to be built or originated, the creative drive must be there first. Once they had been invented wireless and conventional phones would continue to undergo incremental improvements—but that process of gradual evolution alone would never lead to the development of the cellular phone. Without a person to envision and then attempt to create the cell phone, years, even decades might have passed before its invention.

Education works much the same way. We've been hearing much recently about the "effectiveness" of educational programs and approaches, and that is a valid concern if you're talking about education for something like a driver's license, where there's a clearly defined set of skills and goals; but the main goal of education in the general sense is to cultivate and make the most of the latent potential of individuals and organizations. In today's world, a straightforward nose to the grindstone approach to education will ultimately only lead to exhaustion.

Even countries like China and Korea, where entrance exams are even more important than in Japan, many university grads still find themselves jobless after earning their diplomas, and even in America, where the top business schools act as a magnet for the world's most ambitious, students are having difficulty landing the jobs they've worked so hard to attain. Education based simply in hard work only lands students right on the frontlines of the most intense competition, and the whole institution is already beginning to crumble. The only answer is for people to spend time identifying and developing their own hidden strengths and talents; education needs to provide both light in the form of showing people the way, and heat in the form of warm and nurturing support. There is no other way to bring people up so that they can be self-sufficient and strong.

Both in Japan and around the world, on the surface it looks like people are knuckling under to the forces of oppression and doing just as they're told, but there are many who are only waiting for the chance to break free and build anew, and their numbers keep growing with every passing day. You could say that the people of Japan today are like the *kakure* Christians, who maintained their faith during a purge in the early Tokugawa period, although the Koizumi government and the media haven't seemed to notice the resemblance yet. A place where the ordinary person can find a job, work an eight-hour day five days a week, raise a family, enjoy retirement—that's the way society should work in Japan. What we're talking about is a nation in which normalcy means livability.

Now the country needs to come up with and implement actual realistic strategies for production, education and welfare that will make it possible to achieve that set of goals. American manufacturing is already dead on its feet, and the government and economy have both decayed to the point of corruption, and to top it all off, they've declared war on the Islamic sixth of the world's population—by this point they're past redemption. Japan's bureaucrats and politicos surrendered ten years back and now just do exactly what their American overlords tell them. But even so, wealth and value remains within Japan.

The Koizumi regime and the government that the media has created may seem mighty, but it's all smoke and mirrors. The reality is a bunch of weeds that has been drifting rootlessly for the past decade. By simply ignoring the Koizumi circus and the DPJ and stirring things up, we could have a Japan insulated against American influence like it was in the 1950s and 60's and a new Japan was arising from the old. It won't be long before all this great energy takes form. Of course, that's not to say that there won't be confusion here at home in the days to come. Many Japanese concern themselves with tiny problems, worrying only over the balance sheet immediately before them; a true revolution will leave them hopelessly at sea, unable to think or act. Only a new generation of fresh and capable leaders can hope to lead us from this morass.

A New Definition of Success

In the preceding chapters, I have laid out what I hope is a convincing and compelling argument for the unsustainability and fundamental unhealthiness of many of the systems that prevail in the world today, both here in Japan and overseas. But I want to re-emphasize that while this may be cause for some alarm, it should not be a source of pessimism, hopelessness or dread for the future. We are living at a crux, a kind of cusp between two ages that I believe will only glance each other in passing, rather than colliding head-on. As the old fades away, the new will just be coming into its own and the twain shall never meet. Most of us, having lived the majority of our lives in a climate of fear and knock-down, drag-out competition, the concept of a non-confrontational transition, indeed the idea of anything other than apocalyptic change, may be foreign. But I say that when the time comes, the 21st century way of life will supplant the previous ways with little opposition.

Of course that's not to say that the delivery will not be uncomplicated; birth necessarily involves some suffering and tremendous effort. But the end result is the introduction of new joy, new life into the world and that makes all the difficulty worth while. In bringing a new, more fulfilling way of life to light and enabling people to interact and work together, both amongst themselves and with their environments, in more healthful, satisfying and enriching ways, the pioneers of the new age will be midwives to a joyous new birth.

But how can this be accomplished, amid the doom, gloom and confusion? I hope to persuade you all that the key will be to re-define success, not because the old version of success is too difficult to attain (I would say that Japan had completely achieved the old version of success by the end of the twentieth century), but because the old version of success is now no longer healthy or sustainable, and in fact may never have been. We need to come up with new ideas about what constitutes success, accept them in our hearts and share them with others.

A keyword can save a country. In the immediate postwar era, when Japan's infrastructure was in ruins its sense of national pride and identity shaken to the core, political, bureaucratic and industry leaders arrived at and espoused the same conclusion that the future of Japan lay in a single concept: modernization. This one word, this unifying ideal became the underpinning for the great reconstruction and revival that saw Japan rise from the ashes to take its place as perhaps the world's most successful economy within the space of 30 years. That single word, "modernize," set the tone and the pace for the country, it brought people together with a shared sense of values and gave them something to strive for together. Modernization was the shibboleth of the day, a ubiquitous watchword that featured in government white papers, corporate mission statements, political manifestos, and, most importantly, was burned deeply into people's consciousnesses. That shared sense of purpose, that common value of modernize, modernize, whatever else, modernize was perhaps the most important driving force behind Japan's spectacular and phoenix-like recovery. Modernization was the definition of success.

That goal has now been fulfilled, more completely than even the most optimistic and forward-looking of the movement's founders could have imagined. Japanese technology is universally acknowledged as world-leading, its infrastructure, from trains to telecoms, operates with a smoothness and efficiency that are the envy of other nations. Walk into any electronics shop and you are assaulted by an embarrassment of choices—sophisticated digital cameras, DVD-Rs, tiny data storage devices the size of a child's finger, and wide-screen plasma display TVs that would fill an entire living room wall. Japan is nothing if not modernized.

But achieving that goal has been bittersweet. With nothing new to strive for, people can quickly lose their sense of direction and meaning. That has been the case in Japan since the onset of the long Heisei slump, the Lost Decade that arrived in the early 1990s. The older generations are reasonably satisfied with their performance and justifiably proud of their accomplishments, but there is little in the way of modernization for new generations to achieve, no great new challenges on that front to tackle. And while maintenance is a noble undertaking, it fails to inspire people in the same way that the sheer effort and excitement of creation and discovery do.

That is why Japan now needs to re-define its notion of success. The country once again needs a shared vision, the same kinds of energy, urgency and shared purpose that will weld the nation together and drive them to even greater accomplishments than those after the end of the war (after all, we will be starting from a much stronger position this time. The new success will not be defined in terms of trade, or monetary wealth, production output or economic winners and losers. It will not be the outcome of naked competition or mad dashes to grab some material prize. These are all things in which Japan has engaged in the past, and it should be noted, it has enjoyed a fair measure of success. But now, while Japan stands at the top of the world, still the number one in global trade, it is time to change tack, to reconsider its values and priorities and to decide for itself again what success truly means.

For my part, I hope that the new definition will center on the ideal of a great collaboration, a mutual effort to ensure lifestyles of health and sustainability (LOHAS) for all. This is a vision of a ten-year transformation of the very foundations of Japan's society and economy, a transformation in which different new approaches are seen as pathways to strength. The first authors of the LOHAS concept were the American sociologist, Paul Ray, and Sherry Anderson, a psychologist. The movement they launched now has a huge and growing worldwide following and LOHAS has blossomed and diversified into all fields of endeavor and walks of life. For those unfamiliar with the LOHAS concept, it might be summarized as "ways of life that soothe the mind and soul, and exist harmoniously with the environment." This simple concept has sparked something of a revolution in the global consciousness, an awakening to the need and desirability of doing things differently than in the past, of caring about and caring for oneself, others and all living things.

The LOHAS way is seen in all aspects of people's lives. LOHAS is organic and pesticide-free foods, natural foods, safe and healthy dietary supplements, the Slow Food movement. It is paying attention to healthcare and personal development, organic based cosmetics and natural beauty products, yoga, fitness, healing and aromatherapy, acupuncture and complementary medicine, psychotherapeutic counseling and coursework, and a slower approach to life. LOHAS can be found in architecture, traffic management, urban planning and building renovation, on streets lined with green plants and trees, in playgrounds and parks that encourage relaxation and play. And again, LOHAS is energy-conservation, alternative fuel sources, recyclable and biodegradable materials, gardening, ecotourism and earth-friendly commuting. New sustainable and healthy approaches to schooling, work, and society are all LOHAS as well. This movement toward Lifestyles of Health and Sustainability is already spreading to every aspect of human life, in every corner of the world. For those who are interested in reading about it in more detail, I encourage you to google it or enter LOHAS as a search term on Amazon and see for yourselves how far, wide and deep it has spread already.

In this day and age, you might say that just the ability to lead a simple life of days uncomplicated by worries and overwork is one of the greatest luxuries one can hope for. Money and power bring sleepless nights of worry over how to hold on to them, and now, unlike in the past, living a life or working a job that runs counter to one's nature is no longer sustainable (in the past, even if a person found himself employed in a job that didn't suit him, at least he would be trained, and make enough to support himself and his family). All that's left now is a sense of exhaustion.

I think that more and more people are starting to realize this. The human world is just one part of the greater world of nature, and it can't be forced to evolve or progress merely by human power. Economics can be viewed as a tool, useful on occasion and to some purposes, but nonetheless subject to even higher forces and laws; it obeys far more often than it governs. The great majority of human-authored laws don't quite fit right—too tight at the waist, too long in the sleeves—and that poor fit means they are poor solutions for bringing happiness and fulfillment to many. Nature has its fair and foul weather, its heat and cold, but if you stop and think about it for a moment, somehow despite all that flux and unpredictability, it provides a means for every living thing to fulfill its life and its imperatives.

The 21st century was born into the legacy of the 20th: globalization and the unfettered competition it has spawned. That unforgiving antagonism and rivalry is seen throughout the world today, preponderant evidence of the utterly untenable approaches to life and work of the previous century. But how are we to prevail over competition itself? The answer to that difficult question may seem strange, but also somehow obvious. I've said it many times already now, but I will say it here again: the answer is not in being Number One, it's in being the Only One. It's in cultivating oneself, blooming and producing the seeds for further generations. It's in finding the right lifestyle to suit one's nature and calling, and living it; finding the right job, and doing it. It's in recognizing one's nature and calling, and taking the time to learn and grow. When people begin to do these things, then individuals, organizations, lifestyles and work, all gradually become unique and inimitable, the very definition of analog. And that will signal the birth of a truly symbiotic society, a world in harmony.

Comprehensive Transformation

Undertaking to live the LOHAS way is means comprehensive lifestyle change, in all sectors and every generation. This is no extremist niche—it is an entirely new philosophy and set of attitudes that I believe is about to transform, is already transforming, the way people think and behave, at home, at work, at play; alone and with others. It is an evolutionary process, which as you know can seem very gradual, even stagnant until the saltatory moment when sudden transformation is achieved.

If you look at any individual aspect of the world we live in, individual products, isolated trends, the change may be too subtle to detect. But if you change your perspective and look across the totality of cultural phenomena and artifacts so that you are able to observe the set of changes that is now unfolding, the true momentousness of the transformation become clear. With the new definition of success, a new value system is being born. And now, those new values are being taken up and ingrained within people's hearts all across Japan, each in his or her own way, each unique in its own right, but all striving toward the same goals of health and sustainability.

If you think about the development of a child, you may get a better sense of what has been happening, almost imperceptibly, these past few years as Japan seemed to slumber and struggle under the waning 20th century value system. An infant grows as he learns, gaining abilities as his brain and body develops even before he is able to express or act on them. If you watch a young baby, it cannot do anything, and the process of learning and development seems invisible as he lies there helpless. But suddenly one day, he rolls over and crawls, a few months later begins to walk and talk, and within a few years is playing, thinking morally, having conversations, learning to read and write and maturing ever more rapidly into full adulthood.

The LOHAS way is still in its infancy, but that is a temporary condition, and if you watch its growth you will be surprised not only by how quickly it is evolving right now, but how far it will have developed over the course of the next decade. The changes in individual people and organizations may seem subtle today, but they are sweeping and broad, like a wave that may roll slowly, but nonetheless is unstoppable and sure in its forward progress.

You may note that while I am describing the growth of the LOHAS philosophy as a coming revolution, there is nothing new about the idea of healthy living or sustainability. That is certainly true. These are ancient and universal values. But the emphasis on these has weakened and slipped from the forefront of people's awareness. Perhaps it is because of the successes of past generations in prolonging life, fighting disease and protecting against the elements, providing food and exploiting the earth's resources, that we temporarily lost a true sense of the fundamentality of these values. What the LOHAS movement is striving toward and achieving though is not simply a recognition of the importance of health and sustainability, but a deep and widespread integration of this philosophy into every realm of human endeavor, accompanied by the abandonment and extinction of unhealthy and unsustainable practices that have prevailed for nearly a century. This is the achievement we have to look forward to; a revolution not of utter newness, but one of ancient and universal truths embodied deeply in people's lifestyles and interactions. It will be a triumph of shared values.

If you study the history of revolutions both failed and successful, the unifying attribute of the successful ones is the collaborative, synergistic nature of their participants. Not featureless drones moving in lockstep, but unique individuals who nonetheless are bound together by some shared purpose, inspired by a vision of a better world, who go beyond and leverage the strength born of their differences to bring about a better world. It is like a child growing in what appears to be a disorganized fashion, but somehow all of those aspects of his persona—his values, his morals and priorities, his work habits and sense of fun—all arrive at maturity together as he becomes an adult. That is what is occurring in Japan today, often under the surface and hidden from sight, but still gaining in force, a coordinated transformation of the national sense of values that is quietly sweeping past the obsolescent ways of the past century and into a new vision of how we all should live. That vision of LOHAS has already taken root and, like a germinal young shoot that has not yet broken forth into the sunlight, is preparing for the day when it will blossom forth in great beauty and bear fruit.

21st Century Values

The idea of LOHAS is broad in its scope and implications, just as information technology has been in its ability to revolutionize business, lifestyles and culture in unpredicted and unimagined ways. A new emphasis on health and sustainability is sure to have impacts and applications in every aspect of modern life. What will that mean for Japan as we move into the 21st century in earnest? What will people aspire to, what kinds of work drive and motivate them, what will they see as success? The wheel is spinning even now, and over the next few years we will see new values emerge.

You may be familiar with town clocks in old Europe, where every hour a new figure or scene appears, marking the passage of time and also giving character to the given hour of day; Age trails Youth, and festive icons follow solemn Industry. That is similar to what we are seeing now—a new age comes on the heels of the old; one actor leaves the stage and another takes his place. To some observers, the whole thing may seem mysterious, with change coming unexpectedly, but if you know where to look, you can peek behind the curtain, look into the clockworks and see what lies in wait. The value in that is that it allows you to prepare for what is about to enter the scene. And, unlike a clock or a staged performance, this participatory theatre; the audience cannot remain passive. There's a second simile I like to use when explaining how the change will come about. It's like the climbing of Mount Fuji. Different people take different approaches, follow different trails on their ways to the peak. But when they arrive, they all find themselves together at the top. People will arrive at the LOHAS way of life in much the same way. They will take different routes, and have different experiences and perspectives as they find their way up and out. But these diverse pathways will tend to converge at a single summit of health and sustainability.

But what are the principles, the values and morals that will guide them on their way? And what will they see as true success? Here, I'd like to enumerate a number of the aspects of the LOHAS philosophy that I think will be the shared value system of the new way of life. I list them in no particular order, and I make no claim that the list is exhaustive. This is a skeletal framework that will be fleshed out by millions of active participants working to build a new world in the century ahead.

The Great Collaboration

If you were to sum up in one phrase the overarching ethic that will guide and inform Japan's leaders in the 21st century, I believe that phrase would be "the Great Collaboration." And so any question of success in the new century will also relate directly back to how successful an activity (meaning a human life, a business, a community or government administration) has been in those terms. The following is a summary of the some of the characteristics of a truly collaborative, truly great society:

1. Living and working as one

By collaboration, I do not mean simply working together to achieve some short-term goal like a profitable quarter or a transient increase in share prices. Collaboration goes beyond the concept of teamwork, which restricts itself to cooperative efforts within a given institution or group, extending across traditional organizational boundaries. This is an inclusive, not an exclusive, process. The collaborations I describe here include the person next door, the town down the road, other companies, other governments, previous and future generations and extend even to the natural world. Collaborations involve not only synergy (the exponential benefits of working together) but also symbiosis (the state of living together in harmony and co-prosperity with other species).

After a long and painful start to the Heisei era, I can sense that Japan and the Japanese people are now looking to turn to ways in which they can synergize and live symbiotically with others within the country and without. The fundamental problem of the previous century was that the distinction between self and other was too strictly observed and used to divide and separate entities and organizations in ways much too absolute. Alliances and allegiances between families, businesses, communities, regions and entire countries were weakened and frequently done away with altogether.

And even worse, the multitude of autonomous agents was then expected to fight among themselves in a battle for supremacy that was equated with a fight for survival. The tension of that constant conflict was unbearable for all involved, and the materiel demands placed an enormous strain on the resources of the world. The very basis of life itself was put at risk by this hyper-competitive system, the antithesis of health and sustainability.

2. Universal symbiosis

A pendulum that has swung to one extreme will always swing back in the opposite direction. The 20th century philosophy has been taken to its extreme limit, and there is nowhere to go now but back. People have begun to sense this already and to renounce the viciousness of naked aggression by states, killshot capitalism and futureless, empty and egoist lifestyles. In the 21st century, people are beginning to seek ways to live in harmony irrespective of geography or generation, ethnicity, nationality or even species. In this symbiosis that transcends both space and time, people look to coexist peacefully and prosperously with others, all others.

This transcendent all-inclusiveness is foundational to lifestyles of health and sustainability, and stands in perfect contradistinction to the territorial and exclusivist chauvinisms of the 20th century. LOHAS is based on the truth that working and living together with others is actually the most satisfying, most fulfilling and pleasurable mode of existence. It is the key to health, the path to sustainability, and a means for preserving the earth for future generations. And because of that great power, it is also the source of great personal confidence and inner strength.

People no longer wish to live in a world where they are expected and encouraged to compete and defeat. They are weary of strife and vying, of go-for-the-throat businesses and militarist states. More and more what people truly want is to be able to live side by side with others, regardless of race, nation or background, and indeed regardless even of species. Plants and animals, all forms of life, fall within the LOHAS ambit. It is a philosophy that truly embraces each and all, and that is its strength. It is born of the realization that it is not enough simply not to be at war with one's neighbors, locked in an uneasy peace. What people truly want is to coexist in deep amity, to live and work with all creation in a mutually empowering and beneficial synergy.

This symbiosis is not limited to the present, either. Recycling, renovation and respect for tradition are all ways of making peace and re-establishing links with those who have gone before, while developing and pursuing more sustainable ways of life are an effort to leave a legacy of goodwill and heritage to those who will come after. It is an incredible thing to think on, this willingness and ability to live in ways that show respect, concern and love regardless of space, time, race or species. This is the true meaning of symbiosis and stands at the heart of the LOHAS way.

3. A new outlook on life and death

The increasingly widespread embrace of the LOHAS ethic is leading people to change their own personal values systems in unforeseen ways. Changes in people's notions of mortality are among the most common and deeply meaningful. In the past, Japan had a deep cultural belief in the afterlife, whether in the sense of continued life after death, or karmic cycles of reincarnation. But the emphasis on modernization in the latter half of the 20th century brought with it a new reluctance to believe in such things, leaving Japan to turn its back on tradition and religious views.

But when the belief in an afterlife is lost, it is almost natural to see life as a transient, materialist phenomenon, as devoid of greater meaning as the passing of a subatomic particle through space. Unfortunately, that existentialist and anomic view has become the norm in today's Japan. People see their lives as a momentary flash in endless darkness—you've got one and only one chance that ends when you die, and there's no sense in laying anything aside for the future. History and tradition are moot, and the future a distant illusion. When the world begins with your birth and ends when you take your final breath, is it any wonder that people become self-absorbed?

Modernist agnosticism and doubt have made it a great challenge to overcome any tendencies toward egocentrism and irresponsibility; the only proven effective method has been fear. But a climate of fear leads to uncertainty and instability, and ultimately to disintegration. But although those enjoying lifestyles of health and sustainability subscribe to no common religious creed (and many of them to none at all), they seem to be naturally converging on a consensus set of beliefs that is completely at odds with the ephemeral, arbitrary and coldly materialist worldview. By learning about and practicing traditional ways and crafts from the past, and by living with a sense of preserving the world for future generations, they embody an ethic in complete harmony with ancient beliefs of afterlife and reincarnation.

The scientific literature is filled with reports of near-death experiences and spontaneous healing, and even an untutored look at the cyclical nature of organismic life and the functioning of ecosystems highlights the connectedness and continuity of living things. By accepting and embracing this aspect of life and afterlife, the LOHAS philosophy can be a source of great comfort to those troubled by the apparent indifference and mechanical determinism of the modern world.

4. The limits of science

If you speak with people who have begun to wake up to the LOHAS way, you will notice that they seem to ask "Why?" less and less. The scientific method stresses the importance of reproducibility, rigor and rational consistency and is built on solid foundations of observable data, or evidence. It is a powerful system for understanding a certain set of challenges and physical phenomena. But in Japan, despite its status as a leader in technology and manufacturing, people are gradually losing interest in drawing away from science, and outright mistrust of science is on the rise.

Perhaps what's most interesting about this reassessment of the value of scientific objectivism and research is that it is not confined to the poorly educated or radical Luddites, but increasingly seen even among the most scientifically informed sectors of the population. Doctors, physicists, economists—people who make their livings doing science of various kinds—are coming to terms to the limits of the scientific approach. They have seen firsthand the need to go beyond those limits in the search for greater, human-scale truths. It's exciting to see that even professional intellectuals, researchers and knowledge workers have begun to acknowledge that, while a powerful tool, science alone is insufficient to the task of revealing deeper insights and adaptations to reality. Scientists themselves recognize that there are countless mysteries that cannot be answered simply by asking "Why?" and scratching away.

For Japan, which has been nurtured a long and one-sided infatuation with science and objectivity, this acknowledgment of science's inevitable constraints is a positive thing, a diversification of perspectives and a much-needed breath of fresh air that may yet help to rescue the country from the dry and secular catacomb of existentialism it had nearly sealed itself into.

5. Feeling, not believing

LOHAS is not an evangelical movement. You won't see adherents thumping sacred texts or even attempting to harangue others with tedious, rationalistic explanations, debates and PowerPoint presentations. They prefer to trust in their own feelings and experiences, decide for themselves what is right and what is wrong and, if they find others who appear interested, point the way to allow them to take the first step for themselves. This is not about blinkered methodologies and the espousal of dogma in pursuit of an equally constrained material goal or quarterly earnings target. It's about feeling first. Feeling, and listening to those feelings, trusting them to lead you away from evil and towards the good. We've been taught to believe what we're told, not what we feel. But you can only find your path to health and sustainability by trusting your heart at least as much (and ultimately more than) your head.

Of course, there is still a place for rationality and the scientific approach. If, for example, products are misrepresented as organic or a dietary supplement does not contain the ingredients its label claims, then a resort to cold, hard evidence can provide the shortest and surest route to remedying the problem. But your senses, your heart and your gut will usually be the truest guides to determining whether some item, treatment or relationship is compatible with a lifestyle of health and sustainability. Issues of product quality aside, people will naturally tend to gravitate unerringly toward the goods and services, and the lifestyles that will sustain them and keep them well. Feeling is more important than believing.

6. Fun is good

One unifying characteristic of the LOHAS movement is that it attracts people who know how to enjoy themselves, no matter they may be doing. Or, perhaps it's that they have found what they enjoy and simply choose to do it. The culture of competition, be it in business, sports or academia, has left many feeling constantly under the gun and sours even leisure time activities. The jungle law of kill-or-be-killed and only the strong survive pervades the 20th century psychology. We even learn it at school. But the outcomes of that hyper-competition are becoming so clear as to be impossible to ignore. The long-term prospects are bleak for any system that applies rigorous negative selective pressure on a population, singling out only a few "winners" and culling everyone else. Call it meritocracy if you like, but the attrition is unsustainably high, and the absolute denial opportunities for the preterite masses makes for a society lopsided and out of whack. Abandon hope all ye who enter here.

The chance for the "losers" in such a system is to compete by not competing. By finding talented able mentors and role models and learning from them the most important lesson—how to have fun while studying and training—even the less gifted can develop themselves and their own natural abilities. I want to stress that again: enjoying yourself is the key. When you succeed in doing something you truly believe is meaningful and worthwhile; work that leads to health, not harm; practices that promise hope for the future, not plundering and wastrel destruction, the feeling of satisfaction and joy is a sweet fruit indeed. Improving oneself just feels good, and more and more people are coming to realize the benefits, not only to themselves, but to the community and even to the natural world.

Who doesn't bristle at the thought of being squeezed into a prefab mold? Who enjoys harsh and arbitrary discipline? The days of defeatism, self-pity, victimhood, abject conformity and masochism are over. They're no fun at all. LOHAS encourages optimism. It smiles on pleasure and relaxation. It's all about fun, finding wherever you go, whatever you do. Let it lead you to your joy. That is the key to health and sustainability. Find it in the heart, the belly before you even look inside your head. Follow your true feelings and you will find that your own natural talents and gifts will grow and blossom without the least sense of effort. Enjoyment is strength.

7. Cultivating seeds

Many people fret and brux over how to survive in the rat-nasty Gotterdammerung of old-style capitalism. They may think it's by imposing harsh strictures and martial discipline, by devious stratagems and cutthroat tactics. But they would be wrong. Learning to enjoy life, and enjoy learning is the only path to true success. If you've read this far, you are probably at least open to the idea, and possibly even persuaded, that the current order is no longer viable. With a little luck and good leaders, Japan will be spared the death throes of the doomed giants as they pass from this world, and although that time will be characterized by great change and unfamiliar demands, it will also be an opportunity for self-realization. Perhaps not everyone is blessed with the narrowly defined set of talents that were required to claw the way to the top of the 20th century heap, but everyone, every individual human being, has some natural ability, some gift or inborn skill. And for the great majority, that skill is waiting, buried and unrealized. The 21st century will ask people to find their own gifts, and to help others find theirs. And the best way to locate that treasure is to follow your fun.

I believe that in any vision of the century to come, education will not mean desks arrayed like production lines, rote rehearsals and exams, and drill sergeant instructors whose first priority is to enforce conformity. The young will be encouraged to learn at their own pace and to realize their own dreams. Teachers will be more like guides, providing stimulation, support and mentorship to those who are still striving to find their own way. And learning will be a lifelong adventure, a perennial source of joy and fulfillment.

Nearly all of us have been subjected to factory-style schooling at some point in our lives. For many people, it is the only experience of learning they have ever known. That is why so many people think of education as a tedious and unpleasant chore. But lifestyles of health and sustainability afford ample time for learning and personal growth of a different sort. LOHAS encourages taking time, working at what you enjoy and savoring the fruits of your successes, no matter how small they may seem. It teaches that it is OK and important to enjoy oneself. In the 21st century, fun is good.

8. The age of good feelings

Why is it that the LOHAS life is so satisfying and enjoyable? The secret is in the expectation that people do what they take pleasure in, and what they do best. It's a whole new dimension to the old adage "Do what you will is the whole of the law." Moving away from serried orthodoxies and towards individual self-fulfillment is not only a step in personal evolution, but a contribution to a social evolution that we are seeing unfold in our own lifetimes. Importantly, every person is expected to find him- or herself; to bloom as an individual, not merely salute and knuckle down. Every occupation and pastime has a place in this new celebration of diversity and rightness, and that freedom to explore one's own potential will yield greater satisfaction to more people than was ever possible under the current social regime.

Diversity and originality are fundamental to achieving sustainable well-being. The LOHAS philosophy recognizes that individuals have their own unique strengths and needs. Difference is the rule, not the exception. And because every person is so very different, it seems more than obvious that every person's definition of success must necessarily be different too.

But uniqueness does not mean isolation. Cooperation, sharing, mutuality and synergy are bywords for the new age. The Great Collaboration is a group effort, not a solitary pursuit. Even as the old era dwindles and fades away, people who have awakened to the vast and exciting potential of the dawn of a new age will naturally begin to make contact, even without seeking, and as with any community, the shared values and worldviews will forge more immediate and more powerful bonds than any corporate allegiance, school tie or old boy network could. Such bonds lead to great things. The synergies derived from cooperation between two likeminded individuals are calculated by an arithmetic in which 1+1=3.

Synergies have downstream effects as well. Finding true friends and soul mates is a source of great and immediate pleasure, but operates on a much deeper level as well. For friends help and inspire each other, congratulate successes and mitigate setbacks by sharing. True friends encourage each other's efforts and give of themselves and their wisdom. The LOHAS symbiosis is not obligation or co-dependence; it means prosperity and shared joy.

About the Author

Naoya Fujiwara
President and CEO
Fujiwara Office, Inc.

After graduating with a degree in economics from the University of Tokyo, where he majored in econometrics, Naoya Fujiwara joined Sumitomo Electric Industries, Ltd. In 1985, he was seconded to the Economic Research Institute of the Economic Planning Agency for two years, where he engaged in macro-economic forecasting and structural analysis covering Japan, Europe and America using econometric models and also studied highly accurate statistical analytical methods. From 1987 to 1992, Fujiwara was responsible for the strategic investment research group at Solomon Brothers Asia, Ltd. There, he played a leading role in computerized mathematical analysis of financial products, particularly that of derivatives and mortgage-backed securities.

With his internationally-oriented background and cross cultural experience, Fujiwara engages in various kinds of financial consulting work, offering analytical studies of financial markets, projections and a thorough understanding of the respective investment opportunities. A renowned specialist on econometrics in the financial and economic communities, he is active in a broad range of business and professional organizations in Japan and serves as chief editor of Naoya Fujiwara's World Report, his company's financial newsletter. Active in leadership education and consulting, Fujiwara organizes seminars around the country.

Fujiwara also teaches economics with an emphasis on current financial markets at Tokai University's School of Political Science and Economics. From April 1993 to March 1995 he was on the staff of the Research Center for Advanced Science and Technology at the University of Tokyo. Fujiwara is a frequent contributor of articles to professional journals of finance and economics and has also written numerous books. In addition, he appears occasionally on NHK's international

Radio Japan broadcast on the program "44 Minutes" to discuss Japanese financial and economic conditions.

Fujiwara is married and has a daughter and a son.

978-0-595-43858-7
0-595-43858-X